CHOCOLATE SOLDIER

Chocolate Soldier: The Story of a Conchie

Copyright © Hazel Barker
Published by Rhiza Press
www.rhizapress.com.au
PO Box 1519, Capalaba Qld 4157

National Library of Australia Cataloguing-in-Publication entry
Creator: Barker, Hazel, author.
Title: Chocolate soldier : the story of a conchie / Hazel Barker.
ISBN: 9781925139860 (paperback)
Subjects: Dover, Clarence.
            Great Britain. Army. Friends' Ambulance Unit.
            Conscientious objectors--England--Biography.
            World War, 1939-1945--Conscientious objectors--England.
            World War, 1939-1945--Personal narratives, British.
Dewey Number: 940.531620924

All rights reserved. No part of this publication may be reproduced, stored in a retrieval system or transmitted in any form by any means without the prior permission of the copyright owner. Enquiries should be made to the publisher.

CHOCOLATE SOLDIER

The Story
of a Conchie

Hazel Barker

ACKNOWLEDGEMENTS

Chocolate Soldier: The Story of a Conchie is based on the life of Clarence Dover, my husband's uncle. I am indebted to his son Paul Dover for sending me the first few pages of his father's diary, which inspired me to write this book. My grateful thanks go to Clarence's daughter June Cobley, her husband Martin and their daughter Abigail, for passing on photographs, letters and information on Clarence.

Many thanks also to my writing groups for their critiques and helpful suggestions.

My heartfelt thanks goes to my husband Colin Barker, for critiquing my manuscript and enlightening me on the correct nautical terms.

Finally, my sincere thanks go to my publisher Rochelle Manners and editor Emily Lighezzolo, for polishing my manuscript on its journey towards publication.

AUTHORS' NOTE

The war diaries of Clarence Dover inspired me to write *Chocolate Soldier: The Story of a Conchie*. Clarence commenced typing the story of his wartime experience, but death claimed him before he was able to complete his book. I have undertaken to complete his manuscript from conversations with him, research on the Friends Ambulance Unit in India and China during World War II and documents and letters relating to him.

Although names of family members and well-known personalities have remained the same, names quoted in the war diary have been changed.

This book is dedicated
In loving memory
Of our uncle, Clarence Dover
Who died in 2001
At the age of 81

PROLOGUE

Nottingham, September 1939

Sirens wailed. The Dover family snatched their gasmasks and darted for shelter beneath the stairwell. Clarence flattened himself against the wall, the bricks gritty on his elbows, his heart thumping. Everyone except Eva— the only girl among them—put on their masks in fear of poisoned gas.

'Put your mask on, girl,' Watson said.

'It'll ruin my hair-do.'

'You don't know what it's like to breathe in poison gas.' His voice rose. 'Do as I say.'

Eva threw him a surprised look and put hers on. She was Watson's favourite child and he rarely used harsh words with her.

Clarence guessed his father's thoughts. One warm night many years ago, he had been restless, and on the way to the kitchen to get some water, he had passed his parents' room. They had left the bedroom door open because of the closeness of the night and his father had been shouting, 'Take cover! Take cover!'

Worried, Clarence had glanced in—he usually wouldn't disrespect his parents' privacy. His father was huddled beneath his blanket with Ada's arms around him. The bed shook with the tremors that passed through his father's body. He'd never seen his father's face so white and pasty. Clarence smelt the sweat of fear as he stopped and gazed at the unforgettable sight.

The scene had brought home to Clarence the horrors of war and helped him visualise what his father had gone through—the shelling, the torn and bleeding bodies, the poisonous gas and the agony of gasping for air while chemicals seared his lungs. Then, later: the shell-shock.

Clarence flattened himself against the wall, and broke out in a cold sweat. *Would the Nazis bomb Nottingham as they had pounded Poland?* He listened for the drone of planes. In his mind, he heard the crackle of flames and smelled cordite. He waited, fingers in his ears, to block out the thud of explosions.

A sound nearby shattered the silence. It came from the youngest of his three brothers.

'Who blew a raspberry?' his sister Eva asked, her voice muffled by the mask, as she looked at Roy.

All eyes turned to the boy as he sat blowing on the flap of his gasmask. His mother reached out and shook him playfully.

His brother, Stan, who was four years older than Clarence, ruffled Rob's hair. 'Stop that.'

Despite their age difference, most people mistook Clarence and Stan for twins, but that day nobody would have been able to distinguish one from the other with the gasmasks over their heads.

Then the all-clear sounded. Watson removed his mask. 'The sirens were merely a drill to teach us what to do during a raid.'

Everyone dropped their gasmasks into the wooden box by the door as they left. Ada sighed with relief, drifted back to the kitchen and filled their cups with tea. Her normally stern face was sagging now, and she appeared much older than her fifty years.

She put her hand on her eldest son's shoulder. 'Next thing they'll be conscripting people all over the place. You're a tradesman, Stan. Better find work in a reserved occupation before that happens and you are sent off too.'

Stan had a certificate in Joinery and Woodwork. 'Perhaps I'll apply for a job in an aeroplane factory,' he said.

She nodded and turned to her younger sons. 'If the war lasts long enough, you might be called up too.'

Doug grinned. 'I'll join the army.'

Seventeen-year-old Eva tossed her head. 'You'll still be sloppy even in uniform, Scrags.'

Ada turned to her. 'Don't quarrel at a time like this. Doug mightn't be with us for long, if he volunteers.'

Clarence nodded and glanced at Eva. One day she may recall this quarrel and regret her words. If a family couldn't co-exist in peace, how was it possible for countries to live in harmony?

For the next three months, the trees were covered with icicles as Clarence trudged home from work. He drew his overcoat tighter around him, shuddering to think of the homeless in war-torn countries like Poland, who had to face the cold without shelter. *Britain is at war, and my country expects me to join the forces and kill the enemy, but I'd rather face a firing squad than take another's life. My faith teaches me to oppose war. Men are not justified in taking up arms against their fellows, except as a last resort in defence of their lives and to preserve their liberty. The only thing I can do is to register as a conscientious objector. I'll dedicate my life to saving lives instead. There are no winners in war. The individual is the loser no matter which side he is on. I don't want to be a loser.*

Clarence quickened his pace. He started as a passing car tooted its horn, warning him to get out of the way. He could scarcely distinguish its presence in the dark. All headlights were darkened by strips of paper to be less visible to enemy aircraft. Their sound was muffled by the fog too. He rearranged his white scarf so drivers could see him better.

Clarence traipsed past the piles of sandbags and windows criss-crossed with paper to minimise the danger of glass splinters. Like a knight in preparation for battle, the city donned its suit of armour in readiness for Hitler's bombs. Was he ready to do his bit?

CHAPTER 1

THE CLARION CALL

Nottingham, February 1940

Clarence rested his elbows on the table and dropped his head into cupped palms. His shoulders slumped. The clock, set in beautifully carved ebony, ticked in the silence like blows. Textbooks stood neatly aligned on bookshelves within easy reach from where he sat, still occupying a prominent position in his room after his five years of study at night school. Clarence recalled how painful it had been to leave school at fourteen. He'd worked at a clothing factory during the day to help support his younger brother and sisters.

But he'd made up for all that now.

He removed his glasses and ran his hand through his hair. The exhilaration he should have from gaining his Certificate in Business Studies was absent. A Bible lay open beside the table lamp, but his thoughts roamed elsewhere. His eyes stopped on *The Evening Post*.

Clarence tried to visualise the consequences of following his beliefs to save rather than destroy lives. Gritting his teeth, he sank further into his cupped hands as gloom enveloped his entire being. He knew his mother's heart would break under the strain if she lost her sons in such a barbaric war. The thought went through him like a cold blade.

He guessed that his father would let him make his own decision, but his siblings were unlikely to see things from his perspective. Perplexed and annoyed, he rubbed his head. *Many want war but little do they know what is to follow. In the end, who would remember those who had fallen, or lost parts of their bodies?*

Dismayed at the thought, Clarence slammed the book shut. Glancing around his room to reassure himself everything was in place, he turned down the bed covers and switched off the light.

Ever since Clarence could remember, his mother would read to the family from the Bible, then from Dickens or some other literary great. Like the proverbial seed, the readings had taken root in his mind. His mother's prayers and Bible readings to the family had led him closer to God and the words of scripture, extolling him to love his enemies and pray for his persecutors— to cherish peace and hate war. He'd read all the literature of disgust about the Great War. The horror and rejection it had expressed ran through him until the thought of killing filled him with revulsion. He had seen newsreels of the Luftwaffe bombing Poland—the merciless slaughter of Polish cavalry by German tanks. The carnage was sacrilege and wanton destruction of God's creation. Newsreels had also shown endless fleets of bombers throbbing above in the skies and cities exploding. *How can I reconcile my Christian beliefs to kill a man and break God's commandment*, he thought. *How can I look into a man's eyes and justify killing him? How much worse if he had the same beliefs as I do and attends the same church? And how can I allow him to commit such a crime by killing me and having to answer for my death? If he tries to kill me and I don't defend myself, that would be equivalent to my committing suicide and breaking God's law!*

Clarence stood on the footpath and stared at the Post Office door. This was it. Ever since February, when he'd heard about the special tribunal, he knew he had to front up at the Post Office and sign on the dotted line, declaring himself a conscientious objector. Dare he register as one? Would that brand him as a coward to family and friends?

He stepped inside where queues of men waited to sign up for service. Some were spotless in their office suits, others in oil-stained workers' overalls, but they all shuffled forward as the queue decreased. Unpleasant body odours wafted towards him.

Off to one side, a surly clerk sat behind a separate counter. This was the man he needed to see. He pushed his way across the buzzing room, away from the others, and felt as though he was severing himself from everyone.

The clerk slapped the form down on the counter and glared at him. Clarence's stomach clenched when he heard the word *coward* bandied back and forth among the men waiting to enlist. He trembled with anger, *not* fear. His lips flattened and his nails bit into his palms.

He signed the document and, with the chanting of *coward* still ringing in his ears, he squared his shoulders, turned to the taunting crowd, then left. He'd show them he wasn't a coward. He too wished to serve his country, but he wanted to do so in ways pleasing to God.

Clarence spent the next week preparing his arguments. At nights, he sat at his desk, his pen fisted in his hand as he pondered and prayed for enlightenment.

When he arrived at the Shire Hall to defend his case, the sergeant on duty jerked his head towards a large room and spat out the words, 'In there.'

'Thanks.' Clarence bit his lower lip to quell the angry word that rose in his throat but didn't quite make it off his tongue, and entered the room where a few other appellants were already seated. He nodded to them, took a seat and, finding it impossible to relax, he crossed and uncrossed his legs. Clarence had already surmised that the authorities may throw him into prison for refusing to enlist. The loss of his earnings would cause embarrassment and hardship to his family. *It might not happen*, he reflected, although the likelihood always existed. *I will not give in, whatever the consequences.*

Clarence threw back his shoulders and mentally rehearsed his answers.

His eyes settled on the others. Why had they chosen to be conscientious objectors? Were they, like him, objecting on religious grounds? A youth bent over, gnawed his nails and listened to a clergyman. They huddled together, engrossed in what was about to happen, the chaplain obviously willing to plead his cause.

A cigarette dangled at an angle from another's mouth; his hands were stuffed in his pockets, his chin stuck out. Clarence tried to sum him up. A communist? He checked himself. It wasn't for him to judge others.

The sergeant appeared at the door. 'Clarence Dover.' His harsh voice sounded like a death knell.

Clarence swallowed hard and rose from his seat.

The sergeant looked him up and down. 'Follow me.' Contempt gleamed in his eyes.

Clarence caught a glimpse of the hardened jaw line and frowning brow before the sergeant turned on his heel and marched through a swing-door to the courtroom. He followed. The door swung back on him and he flung his hand forward to prevent it from slamming against his face.

Five board members sat at a table on a raised platform. On the wall behind them was a large Union Jack. His heart beat faster at the sight of his country's flag. *I'll show them I'm willing to serve my king and country, too, without breaking God's laws.*

His steps echoed on the hard marble floor in the dimly lit hall. Standing tall, he combed his hair back with his fingers, pushed his spectacles firmly in place and surveyed the men seated in front of him. He hoped they would not see his legs tremble. His mouth was dry. He licked his lips to moisten them.

The judge glanced up from the sheaf of papers. 'Your father, Watson Dover, is a guard on the railways. What are his views on your stance?'

Clarence recognised his own writing on the registration form. 'My father has not expressed his opinion. He respects mine.'

The judge flicked an imaginary fleck of dust off the table. 'You have three brothers and a sister. Are they doing anything to help the war effort?'

Clarence straightened his shoulders. 'My oldest brother, Stan, works in essential services. My younger brother, Doug, will be enlisting, and Roy, the youngest, is still at school. My sister, Eva, worked in the fire service. She's now training as a nurse in the armed forces.'

The judge gave a nod of approval and looked at the military officer whose jaw stuck out at a right angle to his rigid body.

The army official leaned forward and struck the table with his fist. 'Then what do you object to? Think the German Government desires peace? Using religion to shield yourself? Can't go into battle? Can't stomach a bullet? Are you yellow? We'll get the bloody yellow streak out of you soon enough.' The medals on his chest swayed like a cobra's head, hypnotising its prey.

Clarence felt as if he were standing before a firing squad. He stepped back and remained speechless for a few seconds. *Am I a coward?* True, he'd always tried to be a peace-maker at home and avoided fights at school, but that wasn't due to cowardice. *Or was it?*

All well-prepared arguments forgotten now, unwanted thoughts swarmed through his mind. Would he be thrown into prison? The man questioning him had the power to do that. Clarence was sure the military representative aimed to get as many men as he could into the army—by any means at his disposal. Tribunals had done that during the Great War and might do it again.

He stepped forward. 'I have long debated my reasons for not joining up, and I refuse to be intimidated. The answer is "No" to all your questions, sir. I refuse to bear arms or to fight, but I'm eager and willing to help my fellow men. To aid the wounded anytime or anywhere—on the battlefield, if necessary.'

The military officer eyed him in unblinking silence before turning to the minister, who took up the cue. 'Are you a Quaker?'

'No. I know they're automatically given exemption, but I am committed to my own faith.'

'Then why don't you join the army? You're healthy enough, aren't you?'

Clarence thought he saw a fleeting glance of admiration in the minister's face. It encouraged him to state his case. He laced his fingers together tightly to prevent them from shaking. His voice was steady. 'For me, to kill would be a sin. War is contrary to the teaching and Spirit of Christ, and I want no part in it. Everything I do should be as Christ would have done. He'd never kill a man. I cannot imagine Him holding a smoking rifle, or wiping a bloodstained bayonet. God gives life. I don't believe I should take it away.'

'But the Nazis are evil,' the minister said. 'Wouldn't you be doing God's work by fighting against Satan and eventually bringing peace to mankind? Can't you imagine yourself as the Lord's knight-in-arms?'

Clarence's jaw tightened and his eyes flashed. 'No, sir. I've considered every aspect very carefully and my conscience will not permit me to take up arms.'

Members of the board whispered among themselves for a few moments.

He breathed an inaudible sigh. What if they turned down his application? It meant that he'd be liable for a call-up and be arrested if he refused to comply. In a dilemma, he weighed the pros and cons. If he *did* obey and joined the army but resisted firing on the enemy, he'd be court-martialled. He'd have to remain in prison for the duration of the war. How long would that be? Two years, maybe ten. He may even be shot. He heard the crack of rifles and smelled the gunpowder. So vivid was his imagination that a wave of pain from the bullet engulfed him.

The labour delegate turned to him and broke into his thoughts. 'What work do you do?'

Not once had Clarence relaxed his rigid stance, despite the pain in his abdomen. 'I'm employed in a clothing factory. I'm also the honorary treasurer of our church. At Sunday school, I cannot teach my pupils about peace if I take other men's lives. Nor can I preach the love of God to people and foster hate within myself. I therefore believe that my duty is to obey God rather than man. God teaches us to love all men whatever the colour of their skin or the kind of uniform they wear.' His words resounded around the hall like projectiles.

The trade union official turned his back on him, faced his colleagues and raised his eyebrows. 'Sincere?' His words were as faint as the whisper of a breeze.

The men nodded and a pause followed.

Clarence's forehead furrowed—his lips a straight line as he waited for their verdict.

The judge cleared his throat and looked at him. 'You must do something to help the war effort. You have one of four choices—to work on the land, join the fire or ambulance service, or act as an Air Raid Precaution Warden.'

'I'm willing to do my Christian duty. I've already considered joining the Friends Ambulance Unit, and I'm ready to start straight away, if necessary.' He relaxed his brows and a faint smile appeared on his face.

'In due course, boy, in due course,' the judge muttered, his voice sounding kinder than at the commencement of proceedings.

After his interview, Clarence picked up a membership application form from the Friends Ambulance Unit and, upon returning home, he went straight up to his room. He knew his mother had swept and dusted his room during his absence because the faint fragrance of lavender from her clothes still clung to the curtains. Tears welled up in his eyes as he thought of her. He loved each member of his family, but he adored his mother. She had always been his shining beacon leading him towards God. He'd prove to her that he lived according to the Bible's teachings.

He tried to visualise the consequences of trying to save rather than destroy lives. Gritting his teeth, he sank further into his cupped hands. A gloom enveloped his entire being. His father would let him make his own decision. What about his siblings? Would they see things from his perspective? He'd like to show them he wasn't a coward. Despite leaving school at an early age, Clarence had already proved he could gain an education.

Please God, tell me what to do. I'm sure the Germans only want to get on with life as I do—to have a home, food and loved ones. We're all the same, no matter which side we're on—ordinary people caught up in the upheaval. Only the national leaders want war. Only You can understand the enemy across the channel, Lord, he prayed. *I don't want people to think I'm a coward or a Jerry-lover, but I wish to follow You in all things.*

He picked up the form that lay beside his reading lamp and grabbed his pen, resolving to post his application the next morning.

CHAPTER 2

THE WHITE FEATHER

Nottingham, March 1940

At Dixon's Houndsgate Clothing Factory, Clarence braced himself for the jibes and jeers he knew would follow when news of his registration as a conscientious objector reached his workmates. Already he was a stranger in another walk of life. He'd met other conscientious objectors who'd been called up, but he was not yet summoned for service. Weeks of torment and suspense lay ahead of him before he could join the Friends Ambulance Unit.

The verbal abuse was not long in coming.

'Will you be joining up, chum?' a fellow worker asked during a break.

The sneer on his face told Clarence that he knew he was a conchie. Clarence shook his head.

'Afraid to die? Perhaps your dad was gassed in the last war?'

'No, killing is against my conscience.'

'That's a fine cloak for cowardice.'

'Leave him alone,' someone piped up. 'He's a good bloke, even if his ideas are peculiar.'

Fellow workers ignored Clarence, huddling together to talk of the German and Russian invasions of Poland. He flinched, lowered his neck and shrank into his shoulders like a turtle. He'd always been well liked by his workmates, and he longed to be included in the conversation as in former times. *Being a conscientious objector doesn't mean I don't care what is going on in Europe. Don't they trust me any longer?*

Within a fortnight of his court appeal, his employer informed him his services were no longer required. Clarence had been expecting to be dismissed from work, but it happened sooner than he'd imagined. He went to collect his wages for the last time.

The paymaster flicked the small brown envelope across to him with his forefinger and glanced away.

Clarence picked up his pay packet, trying not to acknowledge the rude behaviour. 'Thanks, Frank.' He opened it and white feathers fluttered to the ground.

Flushing, he gathered them up without a word. A strong urge to slam the door and stamp out of the accountant's office possessed him, but he choked back his anger and departed in silence. *I may have lost my job and management may think I'm yellow, but nothing is going to deter me from following my conscience.*

Fortunately, not everyone behaved in the same manner. Some of his friends gathered around and shook hands with him before he left.

Their understanding somewhat appeased his anger, but it flared up again on his way home as he mulled over the paymaster's behaviour. A bitter taste rose to his lips. Clarence strode to the bus stop and kicked a stray stone. It ricocheted against a wall and flew back towards him. He ducked. It made him deliberate on his actions for a few minutes. *I must control my anger and get used to being ostracised*, he resolved.

When Clarence returned home that evening, he extracted his money and showed the feather-filled packet to his family, searching each of their faces for a sign of sympathy. His mother bit her lower lip, and his father gazed at the envelope blank-faced. Roy stepped forward, grabbed it with one hand and delved inside with his other one, as if searching for something.

Clarence's jaw dropped. 'What are you doing?'

'Looking for the chicken,' Roy said with a grin.

Doug burst out laughing and clapped him on the shoulder. Feathers flew all over the kitchen like soft snowflakes, and even before they had settled on the floor, the tension in the room had dissipated.

Everyone laughed except Eva. She turned away muttering, 'Serves him right!'

Clarence heard her, but realising his sister was the only one in the family who felt he was behaving like a coward, a slow smile spread over his face as he flopped into a chair. Eva was still young. Perhaps one day, she too would be reconciled to his choice of action—or non-action.

He felt a hand on his shoulder and turned around.

Doug stood behind his chair, his face flushed. 'Roy and I are both keen to join the forces when called up, but I want to say that I admire your courage in standing up for your convictions.'

'Thanks Doug.' Clarence extended his arms and gripped his brother's shoulders. His eyes grew moist as Doug stepped forward and gave him a bear hug.

By the next morning, news of Clarence's dismissal from work had already spread. A neighbour barred his way on the street. Hands on his hips, he looked Clarence up and down. 'All Quakers are good for is porridge.'

Clarence's colour rose. 'I like porridge—it's tasty and nourishing.' *Why can't people get their facts right. I'm not a Quaker, just a conscientious objector. Quakers are members of the pacifist establishment. I'm a first generation conscientious objector, and have to face the brunt of criticism by myself.*

The man pushed past, digging an elbow into his ribs. The pain in Clarence's chest was nothing compared to the affront he suffered from the neighbour. He held desperately to his faith like a shipwrecked man hangs on to a plank.

How would Mary react to his being a conscientious objector? He'd first seen Mary Flintoff at thirteen, when he had first joined the church at Netherfield. How shy he'd been then, never dreaming she'd even look at him. Month after month, he loitered in the grounds, waiting for her to arrive. The sight of her neat figure and dark hair sent his pulse racing. He held back for a moment or two, thinking she'd hear the thumping of his heart. Then he'd follow and sit a few pews behind her. When the fragrance of roses from her handkerchief reached him, his heart would thud again.

Five years later, on his eighteenth birthday, he had bolstered enough courage and asked to be formally introduced to her. After the service, the minister obliged. A thrill had shot through Clarence at the touch of her soft hand, confirming all his longings and imaginings over the years. He knew she was the one he wanted to spend his life with, and insisted on escorting her home.

She lived in Newstead, not far from Newstead Abbey, which Lord Byron had inherited.

'We're proud of our famous poet,' she said, as they walked.

They continued chatting right up until they reached the gates of her house.

She tilted her head. 'Do come in for a cuppa. There's my special sponge cake if you'd care to try it.'

He did not hesitate. 'You know how to tempt me.'

A rosy hue suffused her face.

Later, they sat around the fire with a cup of tea and a slice of cake. He basked in the warmth of Mary's smile, longing to hold her hand and pour out his innermost feelings.

For the next two years, he fostered their friendship, taking every opportunity to sit beside her at fellowship meetings.

The war began to turn quickly. England's soldiers returned to their home shores tired and depleted, fleeing the German invasion of France. The enemy was just over the channel now. Then from July to October the earth trembled as the Luftwaffe flew overhead on their way to bomb Britain's airfields. People flocked to pray for victory in the Battle of Britain, even though no bells summoned them to church. Clarence and his family prayed harder than they ever had.

'Why are the belfries so quiet these days?' Eva asked.

'The pealing of bells is reserved as a warning of invasion,' her father replied.

In the south-east of England, newspapers wrote of people rushing out of their beds to watch vapour trails and dogfights. Clarence read about people dodging spent cartridges that fell from the sky. He knew the RAF wouldn't be able to hold back the bombers for long and he and his family would soon have to start using the air raid shelters.

Within a few days after the raids, Lady Reading, the head of the Women's Volunteer Service, appealed for the collection of anything made of aluminium for constructing Spitfires or Hurricanes, Britain's famous fighters. Ada gathered all the saucepans she could spare. Watson was not idle either. He commandeered his sons to help in digging an enormous hole for the Anderson Shelter. These shelters were capable of accommodating up to six people, and consisted of six curved sheets with steel plates on both sides.

It needed all Watson's ingenuity to ensure the sheets were bolted together correctly.

In his usual boisterous manner, Roy joked about digging a hole just to fill it again. Finally, they tossed the last layer of soil over the shelter, and Ada and Eva arranged the seating, with ample food and water for everyone.

Although the bombs weren't falling in Nottingham, Polish troops and airmen were stationed at barracks near the city. Most of the girls found the Polish aircrew glamorous as they glided across the dance floor with them. They only had eyes for those in uniform, the fighting men receiving all their attention. Eva was no exception.

Ada had difficulty keeping her daughter under control, and Clarence fumed when his sister slipped out in the evenings with her work friends. Once, he grabbed her hand as she was about to sneak out of the house after dinner. 'Where are you going?'

Eva tossed her head. 'None of your business. I never interfere in *your* affairs.'

'You'll only bring sorrow on Mother if you carry on as you do.' He intensified his grip.

'There's a war on, you know,' she said, wrenching her hand from his grasp. 'These men are fighting for *our country*. Go back to your Bible.' She stalked out, slamming the door in his face.

He wanted to rush after her and drag her back, but not wishing to create a scene, Clarence swallowed his anger and returned to his own room. Once there, he bared his soul to God. *War places lives in jeopardy and endangers souls, Lord. This is only the beginning. How will it end? Please give me strength to deal with all the insults and threats I'm to face, and guide me in everything I do.*

That evening, Clarence stayed up, reading far into the night. At midnight, a vehicle pulled up outside their front entrance. He raced to the door and flung it open. A Polish soldier had accompanied Eva to the front steps and was holding her in his arms.

The strong odour of tobacco drifted towards Clarence. He trembled with rage as he stood at the doorway, facing her with his hands on his hips. 'Get into the house this minute! It's too late for any respectable girl to be outdoors at this hour.'

The soldier released her and saluted before striding back to the taxi, and Eva stomped back to her room.

The man's action quenched the anger seething in Clarence's breast. *At least he respected me.*

Much as he wanted to, Clarence did not follow Eva to her room to continue his tirade, but returned to his own room, changed his clothes and threw himself on his bed.

As the weeks passed, the dark clouds of war grew more threatening. Stan found a job in an aircraft factory. It placed him on the essential services list and exempted him from conscription. He was engaged to Ann and had eyes for her, rather than his family. Doug enlisted in the army and was away, training. Boarding school had snatched Roy off to the country, and now Eva was dating Albert Barker, a gunner from the armed forces. The drawcard had been his uniform.

Clarence remained at home, jobless and on the dole. Whenever the postman stopped at their door, his first thought was: *What is he bringing? Will my application to join the Friends Ambulance Unit be successful?*

CHAPTER 3

MANOR FARM

Birmingham, October 1940

At last it arrived, sealed in an over-large brown envelope and stamped OHMS. Had he been successful? His hand trembled as he slit open the cover. The letter requested him to report forthwith to Manor Farm, Bristol Road, Northfield, Birmingham—Dame Cadbury's home. The Cadbury family were Quakers, who trained pacifists for non-combatant duties in times of war.

He angled back in his chair, hands behind his head, looking nowhere in particular. The radio blasted out news of air raids on London, bringing him back to reality. The Blitz had already started in earnest. He slipped the letter back into its envelope. A train ticket fell out. A glance at the date told him that he needed to leave Carlton for Nottingham Central tomorrow. *I must bid farewell to everyone tonight,* he reflected. *No time to lose.*

After packing his portmanteau, he embraced his mother as though he'd never let her go, and he shook hands with his father.

'Have a good ear,' his father warned him. 'Lights in the stations are so low you might as well not have them at all. Stay alert and watch your step, my lad.'

Clarence moved forward to hug Eva but she gave him her cheek to kiss and stood stiff and tense.

He barely had enough time to catch the local train. He raced to the bus stop, and when he arrived at the station, he swung himself up into the carriage.

Nottingham Central was crowded with men in every type of uniform, and the crunching of boots sounded on the sooty platform. He escaped from the hissing of steam and the murmur of crowds, and sank down into a seat in the carriage. The train jerked back and forth before the engine took up the slack and drew away from the station.

Clarence glanced out the window. Everything had changed since the outbreak of hostilities. Even the signposts had been removed to prevent spies from finding their way about.

His thoughts returned to the court proceedings. Despite what others thought or said, he'd been right to follow his conscience, but it gave him no satisfaction. *But now my journey is beginning.*

'Northfield. Northfield Station,' the guard's voice echoed through the train.

In army fashion, Clarence moved swiftly to detrain. The sun had set and he bumped into passengers as he fumbled his way out into the darkness. He stumbled around with a hand held out in front, in case he bumped into someone or something—quite a feat when carrying luggage. As the streetlights had been switched off and the moon had not yet risen, Clarence placed one foot on solid ground before raising the other. He prayed he'd manage to find the pick-up truck sent for him, and headed toward the glow of a lighted cigarette in the parking lot.

Dressed in army fatigues, a member of the Friends Ambulance Unit waited for him. The man threw down his stub and ground it with his boot, before extending his hand to Clarence.

'Jump in,' he said and climbed into the driver's seat after a brief handshake.

Only a thin pencil of light from partly-covered headlamps lit the road. The three-ton Bedford swerved round the corner, but the driver slowed down when twin streaks of illumination indicated a vehicle in front. 'First time here, chum?'

'Yes. What's it like—the training and all that?'

'The grub's a bit plain, but it's not bad.'

'Are we far from Manor House?'

'Just after the next bend. Then you'll see what you're in for.'

With this ominous statement, they swung into the driveway. The lorry thrust the gravel forward before skidding to a stop.

The driver backed into the parking area, then sprang out of the vehicle. 'Join the others and report at the office.' He pointed to a group of recruits lounged near the entrance and marched down the side of the building without glancing back.

Some were smoking or staring at their boots. Others had their eyes on the manor grounds. Cigarette butts glowed on the ground at their feet. The men had obviously been waiting a while.

Clarence rubbed his finger across his nostrils and scanned the men with whom he was to spend the next few weeks, but, in the dark he was unable to distinguish anyone he knew. 'I suppose we should report for duty.'

A tall Scot strode up to him. 'Sounds sensible enough.' He turned to the group. 'What are we sitting around for?'

'Come on, lads,' Clarence said, flashing his torch on them.

His companion held out a hand as large as a leg of pork and about as pink. 'By the way, I'm Angus Macgregor.'

Clarence clasped it. 'Clarence Dover from Notts.'

'Aye. I'm from Dumbarton, just north of Glasgow.' His hand was warm and his grip friendly.

They stepped into the building, unsure what to do next. At the front office, a sergeant wrote down their particulars.

The paperwork took ages to complete. The sergeant sorted them into groups of four, then assigned Clarence to a room with three others—Parry Davies, Angus Macgregor and Albert Perry.

'You'll work together, dine together and share the same quarters. Leave your gear in your rooms and report promptly to the chairman at the lecture theatre.' He jerked his head towards a small outbuilding in the distance.

Clarence gazed across the grounds. The moon had just risen, and its light leapt off the waters of a lake. He distinguished the outline of a large barn and smiled at the thought of a hay shed being referred to as a theatre. He glanced at Angus, who broke into a baritone laugh.

The sergeant remained unsmiling. 'You'll need a sense of humour to carry you through the days ahead. We're within a stone's throw of Bournville Village and the Cadbury Factory, and, at times, you'll get the whiff of chocolate.' His voice rose. 'That's about all you'll get to sweeten your life. Look sharp and report at the lecture theatre in five minutes.'

They hurried to their quarters—a low wooden structure with a veranda running the length of the building— dumped their gear on the floor, and headed for the barn.

Tier upon tier of benches confronted them as they entered the dimly-lit structure.

Angus elbowed Clarence. 'Looks like we're in for a football match.'

A voice echoed from somewhere up front. 'Hurry along and sit down, will you?'

A hush fell and a tall spectral figure introduced himself as Paul Cadbury, chairman of the FAU. 'All about you are cowsheds and stables converted into a lecture room, mess room and gymnasium with the help of our pioneers. They'll be your training officers.'

He then went on to give a talk on the history of the estate and their daily timetable.

'This will be home for the next six weeks,' he boomed. 'We demand respect for all fellow beings, not solely for those within these premises. Discipline is the same as in the regular army.'

A chuckle arose in the room.

Paul paused until the laughter had died down. 'As you are aware, Birmingham is an industrial centre. To the east, Castle Bromwich produces

Spitfires and Lancasters. Barely three miles from us, at Longbridge, is another plane factory. All around are factories producing shell cases, bombs, guns and other essential items for weapons. They'll be targeted by the Luftwaffe. Manor Farm may be hit by enemy aircraft. There are air raid shelters in the manor grounds, but you will need to practise your skills and help the wounded.'

Everyone held their breath, and not a sound could be heard within the lecture room.

'We are considered to be at risk from paratrooper assault, so be on the lookout for parachutes. Tomorrow we will commence training,' Paul concluded. Then he dismissed them.

Clarence spent a restless night with someone coughing. Others talked or made noises in their sleep. At six in the morning, a bugle blared and they scrambled to wash themselves at a zinc trough. After breakfast, they had to wash the dishes and sweep the floors.

The new recruits came from different backgrounds, although the majority were Quakers. A spirit of camaraderie prevailed. Anyone could leave a packet of cigarettes, a wristwatch or wallet on the table and no one would touch a thing. Honour and the desire to save others drew them together. Mutual respect and understanding led to cooperative action. Everyone tried to give his best.

Albert Perry—the youngest among Clarence's roommates—seemed no more than twenty. Although dark-haired and tanned, his air and bearing made him look unmistakably English. About two inches below six feet, he had broad shoulders.

Parry Davies was a stocky Welshman of twenty-four. The dark hair on his arms only emphasised his corded triceps. He had a musical voice and sang sentimental airs from operas and theatres.

Angus was the most unlikely pacifist Clarence had met. About twenty-eight and strongly built, he gave the impression of being a wrestler. The knotted lines of his blue veins pulsed beneath a tattoo of a naked girl.

The sergeant major drilled them as if they were army personnel, and Clarence threw himself into the training, knowing it would come in useful all too soon. One morning, during a simulated rescue operation, Clarence stumbled from sheer fatigue, heart pounding in the effort required to keep up with Angus with whom he was teamed. His friend stopped, seized their 'casualty', flung him over his shoulder and carried him to a first aid station. Then he raced back to where Clarence stood gulping in a lungful of air.

Angus waited for him to regain his breath before they returned with the empty stretcher.

The lake proved ideal for awkward manoeuvres with stretchers and mock casualties. The six week course was even more demanding physically than the one given to the Home Guards, which consisted of old men and boys.

The Cadbury family impressed Clarence. They never shirked unpleasant tasks like latrine duties or asked the others to do anything they themselves wouldn't do. They doused the toilets with phenol, and used their brooms with vigour, as if they were sweeping up the Nazis with them. At lectures, they warned of the hardships overseas—bombs, primitive living conditions and bad food. Above all, they spoke of the scorn they could expect for not joining the fighting force.

The days ticked by for Clarence with no deviation from the traditional routine, except for Sundays—lectures, lessons in first aid, drilling, workouts in the gym and marching. Weekly route marches increased in difficulty, starting with a walk within the manor to around the suburbs. They were to finish with a twenty-seven-mile bike ride to Stratford-upon-Avon.

On the day before their ride to Stratford, the sergeant ordered them into the lecture theatre. 'You'll be doing ambulance relief work with the army, so it's imperative to keep up with them and arrive at your destination,' he warned. 'People rely on you. As soon as training is completed, you'll be posted to target areas.'

When the session ended, the volunteers gathered on the lawn outside.

'Sounds ominous. What are target areas?' Clarence asked his chums.

Albert inspected his well-manicured nails, on which the half-moons stood out clearly. His blue eyes were in sharp contrast with his tan, but matched the sky as he gazed upwards. 'Target areas mean places targeted by bombers, and for most of us that means London.'

Parry raised a hand in protest. 'Wait for our final briefing. Things may not be as bad as you expect.'

'We're to become targets.' Angus placed his open palm on Parry's head.

Parry knocked it off with his clenched fist and shouted, 'Oh, shut up, you mad Scot.' His jaw tightened and his caramel-coloured skin showed a tinge of pink.

Clarence sized up the situation, realising that Parry had mistakenly taken the Scot's playful manner for a patronising one. 'Tea's up,' he said, hoping to avoid further discord. He strode towards the canteen and the rest hurried after him.

The building was a recently constructed tin shed filled with several long tables and wooden benches. Parry's temper had cooled by the time they reached the canteen, and the four roommates poured themselves tea from the urn, then congregated in a far corner. Clarence cradled the enamelled mug in his hands and let the steam rise, breathing in the aroma.

Nev, who shared the room next to them, dropped into a seat beside him. 'Ever been to Stratford?'

'My relatives live there. I remember visiting the place as a child,' Clarence answered.

Albert stroked his chin. 'How long will it take to get to Stratford?'

'Perhaps a couple of hours. Sarge says we'll have some free time before returning. Would you lads like me to show you around Stratford? *Twelfth Night* is on at the Shakespeare Theatre. We'll get a discount if we go in a group.'

'I'd appreciate that,' Clarence replied. 'What about you chaps?'

All reached for their wallets, eager for entertainment after nearly six weeks of intense training.

The following day, a wonderful morning rose slowly out of the mist. Cobwebs spangled with dewdrops gleamed in the sun. Cycling past the Holy Trinity Churchyard and the adjacent Bancroft Gardens, they headed down to the River Avon. The fresh fragrance from the herbaceous borders in the parks drifted to Clarence, reminding him of his mother's garden back home. Wrens, robins and linnets serenaded as they cycled past.

The long bike ride did not leave much breath for conversation. Once at their destination, they threw themselves on the lawns, smoked their cigarettes, and let the sun dry their sweat-drenched shirts.

Between puffs, Angus asked Nev, 'Why did you decide to register as a conscientious objector?'

'The tribunal of five old gents called me a Christian anarchist and were concerned about my misguided youth,' Nev answered with a chuckle. 'They registered me as a conchie, and here I am. What about you lot?'

'Life is God's gift to man,' Clarence said. 'We don't have the right to take it.'

Angus lit a second cigarette, threw away his match and blew a double shaft through his nose. 'I follow my conscience.'

Albert stubbed out his fag. 'Really now?'

'Why did you join?' Nev asked, turning to Parry.

Parry cracked his knuckles and replied in his staccato voice, 'Thought the army was glamorous, but realised I'd have to kill young Germans my age. Never considered that before. Applied for membership in the FAU.'

Clarence was the only non-smoker in the group, and the smoke annoyed him. 'Well, I'm peckish. How about a bag of chips?'

For a few wonderful hours, they escaped from talk of war and immersed themselves in *Twelfth Night* at the Shakespeare Theatre. Clarence, a keen admirer of the playwright, marvelled at the excellent acting and perfect diction of the actors. He longed to have a leisurely walk beside the Avon afterwards, but, as always, duty came before pleasure. He made straight for the rendezvous as instructed.

At six in the evening, the others drifted in to report to the sergeant, who checked off their names and handed each of them a bag of chocmints. 'Compliments of Dame Cadbury for her chocolate soldiers.'

Clarence grinned as he accepted his share.

Angus laughed. 'You don't join us for a drink at the bar or have a fag, but you *never* miss out on chocolate, do you?'

'I'll swap my cigarette ration for chocolates anytime,' Clarence answered.

'Now, steady lads,' the sergeant said. 'We'll be marching back to quarters. Nothing like exercise to keep you fit.'

Parry cracked his knuckles in protest. 'Why weren't we told?'

'Life is full of surprises, lads. You have to be ready for all emergencies. It's only about eight hours. Just put your bikes in that lorry.'

'He's enjoying this,' Angus muttered.

'Silence in the ranks.'

March back? How would he manage? Clarence's feet were sore and he had blisters on his heel. He thought of Stratford— the serene river, the swans gliding on it, the flowers in the gardens, the statues and landscaping, the birds and the perfect weather. If only they had more time to linger in that peaceful haven.

They tramped home through the night, following the bagpiper who led them. When the walk finally ended, they tore off their boots and wet socks, relieving their sore feet of their prisons.

'Let's hit the sack,' Angus said, throwing himself upon his bed.

The others followed his advice, but Clarence washed his feet and wiped them dry before retiring.

The following night the sound of sirens hurtled Clarence and his roommates out of bed. Planes roared above. A German bomber released a stick of bombs that exploded as they struck the ground, rattling doors and windows. Loose metal roofing flapped and clattered. Clarence glanced out of the window as he struggled to put on his trousers. Clouds of dust rose and a jet of water spurted out several feet into the air outside their barracks.

Angus swore. 'The water main must have ruptured.'

They raced towards the scene of disaster, disregarding the dogfights above, the roar of ack-ack guns and the crump of bombs further off. Clarence's tall, slim figure streaked forward like a greyhound, leaving the others far behind.

The fire truck, dispatched within minutes, came slewing around the corner at top speed and plunged into a murky crater of black muck. Clarence couldn't swim and had no idea how deep the hole was, but he didn't hesitate. He scrambled down into the crater. The water reached his waist, and because of the mud, he couldn't see the fire engine or the men until a head bobbed up, gasping for breath.

Clarence called out and when the man stretched out his arm, he grabbed his hand and helped drag him out. By the time the others arrived, firemen covered in mud and dripping with water were scrambling out of the hole. Everyone pitched in and helped them out. Their hands were sticky, dirt dotted their uniforms and their boots were coated with clay. They must have weighed a ton.

'Thanks for your help, chums,' the chief fireman said, once they were safely out, 'but get back to playing soldiers. The army is out on manoeuvres nearby and will haul our truck out.'

It was the recruits' first taste of bombing and they remained silent. Some bit their lips or clenched their teeth, the muscles in their jaws working. The older men who had been through the Great War shrugged it off.

'This is nothing,' the sergeant said. 'Wait till you get to London.'

A tank soon arrived at the scene. Albert raised his arms. 'My, my. Here's the cavalry.'

'We'd better get out of the way then.' Clarence stepped aside as the vehicle backed up to the bomb crater and pulled the fire engine out of the mud.

They lingered, watching the soldiers until one of the tank crew made a rude sign and called out, 'Goodbye yellow bellies. Too afraid of joining us? Would you like to admit it before we part?'

Clarence bit his lip.

Angus spun on his heel, his face taut and white. 'Come on, chums. There's a bad smell here. Let's not hang around anymore.'

After six weeks of training, the Friends Ambulance Unit ordered their newly-trained members to report for work in London. All were given leave to visit their families first.

Before joining the FAU, Clarence had felt isolated because of his stance towards the war. He'd been sick of being asked when he was going to join up. Now, provided with a network of support, he was ready to face future ordeals. He and his friends had come to know one another's faults and habits but they had grown attached to each other. His confidence was revived. It was time for action. The time to prove himself.

He thought of Mary's last words to him, 'There's no need to see me home.'

His temper had got the better of him then, and they had parted in anger. His heart sank. Now, on his last day at Manor Farm, he debated whether to contact her and let her know he'd be home before he left for London. If he did write, she may think he'd weakened in his decision. Mary considered him a coward. He was yet to prove he was nothing of the sort. He decided to first prove he wasn't a coward in *any* way.

Clarence refrained from writing, hoping she'd realise that nothing anyone said would stop him from doing what he considered to be God's will.

Once his calmness returned, he phoned his mother to inform her of his leave. Then he threw himself upon his bed and dreamed of home. It would be good to be back again, he reflected, if only for a few days.

CHAPTER 4

NOTTINGHAM

Nottingham, 21 November 1940

Soon after Clarence pleaded his case as a conscientious objector before the Tribunal, he had asked Mary if she'd take a stroll in the Abbey Gardens with him. They walked in silence until they reached the park.

His heart thudded as he led her to a seat near the cascading waterfall. He gazed into her eyes. 'Mary, I've just been before a Board of Inquiry to defend my position as a conscientious objector.'

She started. 'That will have repercussions on your family!'

'No. It shouldn't affect them in any way.' He blurted out the words, but he had yet to convince himself that his loved ones wouldn't suffer because of his actions.

Clarence sensed her disapproval as she moved away from him and placed her hands on her hips. 'I'm joining the Girls Training Corps in preparation for entry into the women's military services.'

His blood ran cold as he struggled to follow her thoughts. Was she implying he'd acted out of cowardice? Did she think he feared to endanger his life? None of his family—apart for Eva, whose prejudice stemmed from an immature and carefree attitude towards soldiers—openly objected to his pacifism. If they could accept his choice, why couldn't the woman he loved take him as he was?

His jaw clenched. He controlled himself with an effort. 'I'd never do anything to cause you embarrassment, Mary.'

He leaned forward and clasped her hands in both of his. He recalled his sister and the incident with the Polish soldier. *Was Mary also partial to men in uniform?* His hands shook with suppressed irritation. He tightened his grasp on her to control the shaking. For years, he had placed her on a pedestal and adored her from afar.

The shrill cry of a peacock broke the silence. *Was it an omen?*

Mary withdrew her hand, and rose from the bench. She stood tall and straight. A tendon twitched in her neck. 'It's growing dark, I must return.'

Clarence detected a look of disdain in her eyes as she stepped away from him. He got up and gave her his arm to escort her back.

She shook her head. 'There's no need to see me home.'

Clarence took his dismissal as a rebuke. He did not deserve this. It was all too sudden, too abrupt. For years he had adored her, reluctant to reveal his feelings until he was capable of supporting a wife and family. Now she rejected him.

He crossed his arms, unable to bring himself to plead for her understanding. People were either for him or against him. A vein in his temple pulsed madly. He must have the last word. 'No one can stand between me and my conscience, and you are free to follow yours.'

Mary strode away without turning back, her head held high.

Clarence stormed off. For days he seethed. He tried to forget her, but her image kept floating back to him; her tall, slim figure, the soft touch of her hand, the low voice sounding like a caress and the way she used to look at him. He could not stop loving her.

In pre-war days, the train had taken about an hour from Birmingham to Nottingham, but today, the journey lasted twice as long due to the number of passengers and unscheduled stops.

His father, Watson, who was on duty at the time, met Clarence at the station. 'The six-week training has done wonders for you, son. Your complexion is fresh, and even your handshake is firmer.'

Clarence's face grew hot. 'Thanks, Dad.'

The drive did not take long, and soon Clarence had his mother in his arms. He hadn't ever been away from home longer than a week, and now he'd come back before leaving for London. The house had never felt so empty and quiet; the clock ticked away in the background.

Ada wept as she hugged him. Her sobbing didn't die down for several moments. When her sobs finally subsided, she dried her eyes and put the kettle on. While the tea brewed, she led Clarence out into the garden to show him the changes they'd made during his absence. 'Now I use every square inch for growing vegetables, breeding rabbits for food and keeping poultry.' Regardless of their situation, she always made the most of it. He hoped he could remember to be like her whenever things got tough.

He picked a few blades of grass from the pocket-sized lawn just below their back steps—the only bit she had allowed to remain—and watched the rabbits feed.

That evening, Clarence sat in the kitchen as his mother cooked their meal. Her soothing voice was reassuring as always. 'Bacon, butter and sugar are now rationed. Each of us receives one shilling and ten pence worth of meat. I buy the cheaper cuts and manage to stretch our rations. Roy is more fortunate. His boarding school is in the country and the groundsman grows all the vegetables they need.'

Somehow, she managed to produce five omelettes from just one egg with the help of flour and baking powder.

'You're a genius, Mum. How did you manage it?'

She smiled, and wiped her hands on her apron. 'I've learned to be a magician.'

Her words wrenched his heart. He realised her dread of what present hostilities would bring. Like thousands of others, she'd been through the Great War. If only he could help her.

Later that night, back in his old room, Clarence glanced around to reassure himself everything was in place. Satisfied, he turned down the bed covers, removed the warming pan that his mother had filled with live coals. He had slept under his blue eiderdown since his boyhood days. The quilt felt warm and he snuggled down like a chick beneath its mother's wing.

'How about the lot of us going for a picnic, son?' Watson asked, the following morning. 'I was thinking of Sherwood Forest. What do you suggest?'

'That would be fine, Dad.'

His parents squeezed into the front of the black Austin, while Clarence, Roy and Eva crowded into the back seat. They remained silent, trying to settle down into the small space. His father had used his precious petrol coupons and siphoned off some of the fuel he'd stored in the garage for this momentous occasion. Watson's knuckles turned white as he gripped the steering wheel and drove towards the forest.

Clarence guessed he was thinking of the Great War and all the sufferings he'd been through. His mother turned and looked at Clarence as though to check whether he was really there. She reached over and stroked his forearm. Her hands trembled and the corners of her mouth drooped.

He leaned forward and gave his mother's hand a squeeze. Then he turned to his sister. Eva wore a blue sweater and, on her feet, the pair of wedge shoes, which were in fashion during the Blitz. Rolled up tightly in a victory roll, her hair sported an upswept curl at the top. She fingered her ring—her thoughts obviously elsewhere.

He struggled to find the right words to say to her and, unable to think of anything, he remained silent. Would she continue to disapprove of his views as Mary had done? What was it about a uniform that women went crazy over?

Roy sat in the middle, his hands on the front seat. He glanced back at his brother every now and then. Clarence smiled, hoping the war would be over before Roy was old enough to be called up for service. He enjoyed the comfortable silence as they drove, happy to be in their company.

In Sherwood Forest, the sturdy oaks covered them like a protective mantle. A gentle breeze rustled the few remaining leaves above. Like coloured parachutes they floated down, leaving the tree stark bare. Clarence glanced up at the falling leaves. *Unless a bomb scores a direct hit and destroys the trees, their branches will turn green again in spring,* he thought. *Our spirits are low now but perhaps we, too, will be full of joy once hostilities are over.*

He and his brother, Stan, who had followed on his motor bike, spread a couple of blankets out on the forest floor. Others brought the food baskets and bottles of lemonade from the car. They laid out the plates and cups, the tomato sandwiches, the lettuce hearts and cream crackers.

Clarence reached out and took a sandwich from a wicker basket. The lovingly-prepared snack tasted like sawdust as his thoughts lingered on the possibility of one or all of them not surviving the war.

He saw his mother's eyes on him. He smacked his lips and flung an arm across her shoulders. 'Your food is delicious, Mum.'

Eva chose her sandwich carefully, as if to check whether it contained her favourite filling.

'You look half-starved—' Roy started to say, but he stopped when his mother glared at him. He ate his sandwich in quick bites, swallowing the bread before he chewed it, talking with the food still on his tongue.

They sat munching their lunch and remembering past times. When the evening shadows grew longer, they packed their things in the car and drove home in silence.

A lump rose in Clarence's throat. *Will the good old days ever return? Is this the last time we'll be together?*

On the final day of his leave, Clarence and his parents went to Ye Olde Jerusalem Inn.

'This is where the crusaders used to stop on their way to the Holy Land,' his father said. 'You, too, are about to embark on a mission, son. Whatever you consider right is what the Lord wishes for you.'

Never before had his father bestowed his blessing on Clarence's choice for non-combatant duties. Watson hadn't voiced disapproval, but now that Clarence was leaving for the war zone, he must have realised his son was not a coward. His tacit approval gave Clarence a lift. The sense of being an outcast—disliked and ridiculed—was one of the greatest crosses he had borne, but his father's blessing strengthened and cheered him.

After the meal, Clarence and his parents visited the gardens of Nottingham Castle. They spoke less now, finding it difficult to talk about what was on their minds without choking with emotion.

'Take care, son,' his mother said when Clarence was about to leave. 'We'll be praying for you. I know you'll read a passage from the Bible every day.' A few unshed tears hung on her lashes.

They embraced.

Watson displayed a stiff British upper lip and clapped Clarence on his back. 'Don't take any unnecessary risks, son.'

Clarence swallowed hard, knowing that even though he had not joined the army, the possibility of getting killed loomed just as high.

***

Meanwhile, Mary sat alone at home and thought of Clarence. A pleasurable feeling rose in her stomach like butterflies fluttering their wings. Apart from his views on war, they had so much in common. She reminisced about their days in the Fellowship of Youth when they had attended the National Church of Christ Conference every year and arranged outings and holiday camps. Was it fate that had drawn her to the tall blond boy even as a young girl? She knew she'd never forget him.

Friends had seen him in Nottingham, and she hoped he'd drop in, despite their quarrel over his registration as a conscientious objector, but he didn't show. She berated herself for not going to see him when she had the chance—and for not telling him she was sorry she'd caused the quarrel. The thought that she might never see him again tore her heart in two.

***

Watson dropped Clarence at the station and after a hearty handshake, he left for work.

Clarence stood silently, waiting for the train—no longer regular as in former days. Crowds brushed past him as his mind wended its way to Mary. She was probably practising her Morse code or map reading. Doubtless, she considered him a weakling. Well, he'd show her he was no coward. *Everyone dislikes cowardice but why do some people think it noble to disregard the value of life—one's own and that of others?*

His heart clenched at the thought of not seeing her again—never hearing her sweet voice, or touching her soft hand. He longed to tell Mary of his love for her, to crush her in his arms and prove he was as brave as the rest of them. Would his work in London during air raids be sufficient proof he wasn't a weakling?

CHAPTER 5

THE BLITZ

London, 28 November 1940

St Pancreas Station was a conglomerate of activity as the Nottingham train wheezed to a stop, disgorging passengers. From the moment Clarence's foot touched the platform, the crowd jostled him towards the entrance of the station and the bright red bus outside St Pancreas whisked him away.

How different London was from Nottingham. Heaviness lay on his chest as he stared at the smoking heaps of rubble, smashed windows and sagging doors. Sandbags were piled up before public buildings to protect plate glass from shrapnel. Statues had been removed or hidden behind timber. Air raid trenches lay in readiness along gutters and in parks. Homemade humped-back shelters crouched low like tortoises in tiny gardens. Taut cables held barrage balloons aloft in mock celebration. These great silver elephants in the sky prevented bombers from flying too close to their targets. Beneath them, convoys of army trucks and trains, laden with the projectiles of war, rattled along to places unknown. Pavements rang with countless feet—mainly the heavy boots of soldiers from all over the world.

The Blitz had commenced on the evening of the seventh of September, when three hundred and forty-eight bombers and twice as many fighters followed the Thames up to London. Like vicious wasps they had deposited their burning stings on the city and blasted it for two hours, while Britain's aircraft were away safeguarding the coastal airports. The bombing had continued until four-thirty the next morning.

Despite all the loss of life and turmoil, life in London still carried on with dogged determination. People went to the cinemas, football matches and races.

Clarence's heart ached at the sight of bombed buildings. Anger against the enemy seethed within him. How ruthless they were! Did the pilots gloat at the death and destruction they caused, or did they, like him, shudder at the loss of lives and limbs?

In less than fifteen minutes, the bus deposited him and his portmanteau before the hostel, a large brick building in Philpot Street. Bemused, he stood staring at the place that was to be his temporary home.

At the reception office he received directions to his room. No familiar faces met his gaze. His roommate had already left for work. Those on day duties and night shifts shared beds—his was warm from the former occupant. A shirt, reeking with stale perspiration, hung on a clothes hanger. A soiled handkerchief, probably dropped from the garment, lay on the floor. He picked it up with two fingers and stuffed it back into the shirt pocket.

Clarence bit his lip and unpacked his portmanteau. Taking out a framed photograph of his family, he placed it on his half of the bedside table. Then, wiping imaginary dust from the glass, he replaced it at another angle. The photo gave some semblance of home.

He stroked the worn cover of his Bible. It had been a gift from his mother. Should he read a book before dropping off to sleep? He was about to change into his pyjamas when sirens screamed their painful message.

Not knowing where the shelters were, he hesitated. The ground trembled with the thunder of aircraft, leaving him dumbfounded and unable to move. So this was the Blitz!

Within minutes, the screech of bombs rent the air. Clarence rushed out of his room into the hallway. *Where were the air raid shelters?*

Amid the trampling of boots and loud voices, someone called out. 'We're going up to look at the fireworks.'

Clarence stood still. *Fireworks? What does he mean?*

'Well, are you coming?'

Everyone near him ran up the stairs. He joined them. Three flights more to go. They tumbled out on to the roof.

'Over this way,' a voice called.

Clarence followed. Out on the parapet, the crackling of fire and the yells of rescue workers reached him. From the ground, flames shot hundreds of feet into the air. The sky turned red and angry immediately above the fire. Overhead, a pinkish-white puff, like fairy floss, blossomed in a great cloud. The Tower, Houses of Parliament and Nelson's Column were prominent features of London. *Where were they?*

Even from where he was, the air was saturated with the smells of dust, smoke, cordite, sewerage and leaking domestic gas. His vision blurred. He blinked hard and rubbed his eyes. St Paul's massive dome floated before his gaze like a battleship on a sea of fire. The sight held him spellbound. Clarence remained rooted to the spot. His face turned ashen and he broke out in a cold sweat. The panorama of the city, magnificent with its backdrop of red and yellow fingers reaching for the sky, tore at his heartstrings. Centuries of history, of glory, fragmented before him.

His legs felt weak but he fought his fear. Soon his fear gave way to anger. Clarence balled his fists. 'How many of us do you want to kill before you're satisfied?' he shouted. Then he thumped his fist on the railing. 'Insanity.'

'Malevolence, not madness.'

'Pardon?' His eyes shifted from the flames to the rooftop where they had gathered. Clarence blinked to clear his vision and distinguished a man who stretched out a hand towards him.

'By the way, I'm Jack.'

'Clarence.' He extended his hand. 'I arrived late afternoon. Haven't met anyone I know—yet.'

'You'll get to meet everyone, and if old Adolf has anything more to do with it, you'll never forget London.'

'Is it like this every night?'

Jack shrugged but remained silent.

'Can't distinguish London's landmarks from up here,' Clarence continued.

'With the blackout and all, you usually can't. Right now the smoke and flames are hiding them.'

'Surely no one can be alive in that,' Clarence whispered. 'Looks like hell itself.' The sound of fire engines racing from street to street reached him. Something that appeared like a piece of burning paper hurtled in his direction. He ducked. A pigeon flew past, wings in flames. Clarence shuddered. Ever since he could recall, he had had a dread of fire. Perhaps because of the pictures of hell his mother had shown him and paintings of the Great Fire of London he'd so often gazed at in history books.

'You'll have to ignore the carnage, grit your teeth and get on with the job.'

'Is it possible not to be moved by the sight of torn and bleeding people?'

'It's got to be done, lad,' replied Jack. 'Got to be, or we'd stand around moaning and not get on with helping those we can.'

'The sight scares the life out of me. I don't know how I'll manage.'

'Only remember your training.'

'They never trained us for this.' It was the most hateful sight he'd ever seen, and the memory remained to haunt him forever.

At lunchtime the next day, Clarence was reunited with his friends, Angus, Albert and Parry. Men no older than him allocated jobs to them. Jack Skurr, who Clarence had met the previous day, assigned Parry to London's East End for hospital duties in a county council hospital, and sent Angus and Albert to work at the rest areas.

Before departing to their respective spheres of duty, each member received two khaki uniforms with the letters FAU on the shoulder badges.

'Be prepared,' Jack warned them. 'Air raid sirens scream out nearly every evening at seven. Then those of you on night shift remember to fasten on helmets, and don't forget to take your gas masks before leaving for your designated posts.'

Clarence was posted as a medical orderly in the geriatric ward at St Alfege's Hospital, Greenwich. The day he reported for duty, he had to help patients to the Greenline buses lined up on the road for evacuation to Exeter.

A perfect specimen of senile decay panted and wheezed as he hobbled along with unsure steps. 'I'm comfortable here,' he said. 'Where are you taking me?'

'Where Nazi bombs won't reach you,' Clarence answered. 'You'll love the fresh air and the green fields in the countryside.'

The shrunken lips trembled and a tear trickled down a groove on his face. 'What is there to live for anyway? They'd be doing me a service, you know.'

Clarence stroked the man's hand and helped him into the bus, taking care not to hold him too firmly, lest he leave a bruise on his parchment-like skin.

Not long after the evacuation, ambulance workers brought in a wounded air raid precaution warden. Shrapnel had hit his thigh and entered his abdomen.

Clarence shaved the patient's stomach and assisted in the operating theatre. Wet sucking sounds arose as the surgeon pulled out the intestines. They squirmed like a mass of worms, while he searched for bits of shrapnel. An odour of vomit filled the room and a sour taste rose in Clarence's mouth. His stomach lurched, but he swallowed hard. *It won't do to spew all over the man's guts.* He averted his eyes and glanced at the white wall opposite him. A fly, attracted by the odour of blood, crawled up, waiting to feed on the feast.

The distraction helped his nerves to settle.

The surgeon sewed the last stitch in the wound and straightened up with a satisfied look.

Days later, Clarence visited the wounded ARP warden, who now sat up in bed. 'How are you, chum?' he asked, thinking how resilient the human body was.

'Doing bugger all,' the patient replied, with a broad smile. 'Doc says I'll soon be back at my post.'

'He's done a great job. One minute you were on the table, then, Bob's your uncle, he'd sewn you up.' Clarence held out his hand. 'Take care. Won't be seeing you again. This is my last day here. I've been delegated to fire-watching duties.'

Daylight was fading as Clarence boarded a bus that lumbered to his hostel. He ascended the stairs, wondering what his new work would entail. He'd been trained for ambulance duties, not this.

The FAU had transferred Angus from the rest areas for a spell, and he sat waiting by the entrance. Clarence was glad to be rostered with him once more. They were expected to extinguish incendiaries that fell on the roof, or to summon help if a conflagration arose within an allocated area.

To fight the fires, they received a stirrup pump, which had a footrest and a long hose with a nozzle attached. He was mainly involved in watching where the incendiaries landed, then reporting them to the fire stations. He and Angus took turns, climbing up to the lookout tower with a bucket of water, in case of a fire. There, they would hunker down in a small concrete pillbox on the roof. Cylindrical in shape, it provided a safe place from shrapnel and machine-gun fire.

Angus went on lookout duty first. Amid the bombing, the bursting of anti-aircraft guns and the crackling flames below, he indicated the spots the bombs had fallen. Clarence waited below until Angus shouted out the precise position of the blaze. Then he raced to the phone and relayed the information to the nearest fire station.

Two days after the Christmas of 1940, when Clarence was on fire-watching duty, the sirens screamed again. Minutes later, planes roared overhead, dropping incendiaries. The falling bombs sounded like whistles.

At times, they had a loud tearing sound. The sky glowed with flares suspended on parachutes, floating to earth. Firebombs fell in nearby streets.

Men grabbed their first aid packs, stirrup pumps and pails, and rushed from the shelter of the hostel, smashing doors and breaking into deserted houses. Some doused the incendiary bombs with sand. Others pumped furiously, one hand on the stirrup-pump handle. Their partners held the hoses, directing jets of water from the buckets toward the burning buildings.

Clarence looked down from the tower. Although safe in his pillbox, he trembled and beads of sweat broke out on his forehead. *I must overcome my fear of fire. I must. I must.*

After the flames had been quenched, and the all-clear sounded, Jack briefed them on the night's tragedy. 'The raid has left more than one hundred and sixty people dead, with six hundred casualties and fifty-four major fires. Hundreds of homes were set ablaze and eight Christopher Wren churches destroyed. The Nazis chose their timing carefully when the tide was low and we were unable to draw water from the Thames.'

Clarence shuddered. Soon it would be *his* turn for firefighting down below with the others. His stomach churned and a sour taste rose to his mouth. He wanted to spit, but there was no saliva to expel. Dizzy with fear, he hung onto the rails. He must not faint. There'd been stories of men wetting themselves or soiling their pants through fright, but Clarence never imagined it could happen to him. Now it seemed he was on the brink of losing control of himself. 'Help me, Lord,' he prayed.

Amid the clamour all around, he remembered his mother's voice as she read to him from the Bible, 'For the Spirit God gave us does not make us timid, but gives us power, love and self-discipline.' (Timothy 1:7).

A flush of warmth suffused his entire being. Of course he would be given the strength to overcome all obstacles. He secretly wished he had any other job in place of firefighting, but he determined not to reveal his fear or allow it to overcome him.

A few days later, Jack sent Clarence and Angus to St Paul's Cathedral for training with two expert firefighting teams. That evening, bombers flew over London's icon. An incendiary bomb fell on the roof and half a dozen men were chosen to crawl along the wooden beams with hand pumps. Clarence was selected because of his slim build, and Angus had to remain behind with the others to protect the interior of the building in case the fire spread.

Clarence had no fear of heights, but he braced himself, taking care not to look down. He tried not to think of the blazing bomb ahead—a sheer impossibility because of the crackling noises and the stench of burning phosphorus. Still he crawled forward. A gust of hot air enveloped him as the fire burnt a hole in the roof, exposing the sizzling sparks of blue and white. Drenched in perspiration, his eyes misted by tears, Clarence reached the blaze. Perched on the rafters, he directed jets of water from his hand pump, preventing further conflagration.

The ball of flames burnt through the roof and collapsed into the nave beneath.

Only then did Clarence venture to look below. Angus and the other firefighters were smothering the flames with sandbags. Slowly, Clarence descended the ladder. His heart raced, his breathing came in short bursts and his mouth was dry, but a sense of pride took possession of him.

Angus's eyebrows were singed, and sweat streamed down his red face but they had both come out unscathed.

Jack smiled broadly at them the next day. 'Well, I guess you're ready for anything now after last night's experience. We'll put you on firefighting in another area. It may not be as demanding.'

Firefighting proved a bigger challenge than fire watching. Clarence vented his anger upon civilians who hung around, watching the blaze and putting others at risk. 'What are you doing here? Can't you see that barriers have been placed, warning people not to enter the premises?'

'It's our home. Where can we go?' the people said.

What could he do under the circumstances? It was their dwelling, their life. Overwhelmed by a sense of impending disaster, Clarence soon came to appreciate the incongruity of it all.

Breathless and dizzy whenever he fought fires, he retreated behind a façade of silence.

Around midday, after a shave and a shower, those on night shift gathered for lunch and swapped stories.

'We've adopted a dog,' Clarence said. 'He attached himself to our watch. When the sirens scream, he joins in and howls his head off, trembling all over.'

Albert and Parry, who were now on shelter duties, munched their lunch in silence. The tinkle of cutlery and the loud ticking of the clock were the only sounds in the room.

Seeing the struggle on their faces, Clarence knew they had been through something too painful to discuss. He glanced at his watch. 'Well, if we want a shut-eye before dinner, we'd better do so now or we'll be late for night duty.'

No one needed a second bidding.

After a brief spell at firefighting, Clarence and Angus were assigned to rescue work and ambulance duties. Clarence sighed with relief and thanked God. They reported to their station to find the grey vans and cars parked and ready. Some of the ambulances were old limousines converted to carry two racks of stretchers on either side. They each contained a first aid box with a few aspirins and a roll of Elastoplasts. A pair of canvas flaps at the back served as the door.

Clarence stared at the equipment in disbelief. *Is this all we have for the wounded?*

A week later, the truth of the situation struck home when the casualties mounted. The most he could do was to stop the bleeding, ease their breathing and get them to hospital as soon as possible.

Raiders came every night, sometimes up to three hundred aircraft but never less than fifty. The raids usually began around six in the evening and went on until midnight. Each time, Clarence climbed into the cabin with butterflies in his stomach and started the engine. *Burning buildings still stand, but as I enter, will the walls collapse and bury me,* he wondered. *Am I strong enough emotionally to face the flames and mayhem?*

Debris blocked the roads. The top-heavy vehicle was often in danger of overturning as they sped through the shrapnel-scarred streets in the ambulance. The odour of smoke, brick-dust and high explosive hung over shattered buildings.

On their way to the various London hospitals, Clarence and Angus passed scenes of carnage in streets strewn with glass and debris. Ack-ack guns pounded on as they drove to pick up casualties. Bombs whistled and whizzed down.

The ambulance bounced over a pothole. Clarence focussed his attention on the road ahead. His muscles tensed. Seeing a collapsed house with rescuers searching for wounded or dead, he brought the vehicle to a stop. *Looks like they need help here.* He turned off the ignition, and raced to give a hand.

The smell of cordite, burnt timber and dust rose to greet him, and he started to cough. A badly scorched dog whined and dug among the ruins. *Someone is under the rubble.* He rushed forward, broken glass, crockery, chairs and tables crunching beneath him.

A pile of debris turned out to be a half-buried old man. The dog was licking the grime from his master's face. Streams of dust tumbled from cracks in the plaster behind them as beams were still falling. The remains of the building seemed about to collapse.

Clarence and Angus worked frantically to remove the masonry that held the victim down, lifting each piece and placing it aside. Their hands bled from its sharp edges and dust stung their eyes. Bombs continued whistling down, and they were in danger of shrapnel, but they did not pause.

They finally pulled him out, dusty and caked with dirt but unhurt.

Without thanking them, the old man patted his pet, wiped the grit from his eyes and started to search in the wreckage.

'What are you looking for?' Clarence asked.

'My grandchildren.'

A cold hand gripped Clarence's heart. He knelt and put his ear to the ground above the cellar to listen for smothered cries.

The hound sniffed around—without success.

A lump rose to his throat as Clarence drove on to their allocated spot, picked up a load of wounded and left them at the nearest hospital.

Back at the station, weary from wading through the rubble and from lifting obstacles and casualties, they rinsed the ambulance with buckets of water and disinfectant, finding the combination of dust, blood and vomit difficult to remove.

When finished, they cleaned themselves. Their lashes had grit in them. They removed it, taking care to search for little pieces of glass.

When everything was in order for the next load, the two men sat down for a cup of tea.

The bombing was intense and resources and manpower so stretched that men were forced to catch sleep whenever possible. One evening, after daylight had long faded, Clarence dozed off on the floor of the garage. Curled up beneath dark grey blankets, he dreamed of entire streets burning, houses blazing and people with raised arms crying for help.

The sound of rapid fire in the distance roused him. With a surge of energy, he kicked off his blankets, grabbed his gas mask and put on his tin hat as he ran.

Angus was already dragging a stretcher that normally required the strength of two men. He clamped it down on a rack without waiting for assistance.

Thankful for his friend's vigour, Clarence snatched one end and helped stack the rest. Then he climbed into the ambulance and started its engine, pressing and easing off the accelerator pedal, warming it up.

His knuckles were white as his long, lean fingers gripped the steering wheel.

The booming of anti-aircraft guns grew louder. Overhead, searchlights probed the heavens and a red glow spread across the night sky like a warm blanket.

Clarence detoured around diversions and blocked streets, then stopped in front of a blazing building. Heat penetrated the canvas hood. He imagined the hair on his head scorching.

They scrambled out of the vehicle, but a wall of fire confronted them. The roar of the flames mingled with the blast of bombs and guns. The acrid smell of cordite and burning paint stung their nostrils. Clarence stood still, adjusting his vision to the glare and trying to overcome his dread of being trapped in the inferno. His eyes smarted. Not one house was standing. Rafters plummeted down with a reverberating crash amid a thick cloud of dust and smoke.

Silhouetted against the glowing blaze, men carried hoses and ladders. 'Over here,' a voice called.

Angus ran forward, holding the front-end of the stretcher. Clarence snatched up the other end and stumbled over the rubble. Angus stopped just long enough for him to regain his balance.

After they had loaded the wounded into the emergency vehicle, Clarence clambered into the driver's seat and drove off. Huge bomb craters left only a narrow passage, but he proceeded with two wheels on the pavement, the remaining pair on the edge of the crater.

The nearest hospital was too full and turned them away. He raced to Guy's, nearly colliding with a fire engine. At the ambulance bay, nurses rushed out with stretchers, conveying the casualties indoors, placing them along corridors before sorting them out in order of priority for the operating theatre.

On their return from Guy's, rescue workers at a bombed building waved them down. Angus drove back with another full load of injured, while Clarence remained behind to help.

He crawled through a pile of rubble—bricks and timber interlaced with what had been a home put together over a lifetime of sweat. He stumbled into something soft. A hand clutched a teddy bear. *Where's the body?* He prodded among the ruins. *Another hand.* The fingers protruded from a pyramid of roof tiles. Breaking out in a cold sweat, he seized a twisted iron railing, prised against the debris and exposed the body of a child. The little boy, white and waxen like a Michelangelo carving, was dressed in a sailor suit. His countenance was stained with the dust and grime of the family home.

Clarence stood looking at the mess, the rubble, the row of bodies displayed on the street like fish in a shop window. Then he bent and lifted the child gently, as if life still clung to him. He picked up the arm, placed it on the body and laid the corpse along with the other dead.

The eyelids trembled faintly.

Transfixed, his eyes remained glued to the face. *Is it a trick of fancy or the flickering of the flames around me?* The heat from the inferno could not prevent a cold shiver from running up his spine.

Lips taut, he reached down and felt the little wrist. A vein in his neck throbbed rapidly. In a burst of fury, he longed to get behind an anti-aircraft gun and blow the Nazis out of the sky.

The child's pulse, light and very deep, throbbed slightly in spite of the loss of blood. Clarence was shivering, and the butterflies had returned. Perhaps he could save one life out of so many. *Find the phone box and get medical help. Don't panic. Stay calm. One stage at a time. Be methodical. Do it by the book.* He laid the boy on his side in a recovery position, doing whatever he could in the suffocating smoke. Then he stumbled towards a public telephone booth.

Blown off its pedestal, the red box lay at an odd angle with no roof or door; its square windows smashed. The mechanism choked with pennies from so many appeals for help, refusing to take any more calls. What should he do? Clarence looked around, praying for guidance.

A man stepped out from a GPO vehicle, and told him he was checking the phones. He removed the coins and Clarence put his message through.

Within minutes, an ambulance came. Clarence gazed at the stretcher-bearers carrying away the boy and his teddy bear into the van. He choked back a sob and listened to the decreasing wail of its siren as the vehicle sped through the bombed-out city. He sighed. Perhaps he'd saved a life today.

Exhausted, he sat down on part of a wall, waiting for Angus to pick him up and collect another load of wounded. *What a waste of lives,* he thought. *Why did countries wage war, knowing that death and destruction would follow? Did the commandments of God mean nothing to governments?* Once again, he flinched at the sight of such ruthlessness.

The memory of that day seared itself into his brain like a branding iron. He knew the scene would haunt his dreams forever.

The carnage continued for weeks. Clarence braved the fire bombs and flames, scrambling through the debris, labouring in clouds of dust and suffocating smoke. He extricated corpses, some still warm and intact; others, a bloody mess. Above him, searchlights scanned the sky, and anti-aircraft guns belched, spewing out a staccato of tracer shells at the enemy.

The moan of the air raid siren and the dull roar of planes filled the city from dusk to dawn. Screaming bombs left their signature across London.

Each foray seemed larger than the last. There was no respite.

Every two minutes a new wave would fly over and drop batches of incendiaries. They fell as heavily as hail from a winter thunderhead, exploding with a flash—simmering down to pinpoints of dazzling white. Brilliant flashes from anti-aircraft shells lit up the skies, their pounding mingling with the whine of missiles and loud explosions. Rescue workers scurried along the streets, ambulances screeched and raced to the scenes of carnage.

Everyone did their appointed tasks and helped casualties.

Then it was all over—until the next time. The butterflies of fear persisted within Clarence; the fluttering more subdued now.

After a few weeks, Clarence and Angus learned not to stop and help others, but to go directly to their allocated area as it would only cause confusion. With inscrutable faces, they worked in blazing buildings, rescuing the wounded.

People took shelter in underground stations, but only the deepest ones were safe. Tilbury shelter, consisting of a network of tunnels, was the largest in London. The gates opened at half-past four in the afternoon, but queues commenced from midday, regardless of daylight sirens or dogfights overhead. People huddled there at nights, amid the urine buckets and litters of paper.

At dawn, they could emerge to find their homes a heap of rubble. Scores of civilians flooded into rest centres—the sole option available for the bombed-out population. Some tried to make the underground railway stations their home, but officials sent them off during the day. Others roamed the countryside. Worry dulled the brightness of life.

When the night raids ended, ambulance workers, firefighters and volunteers from rest centres returned to the hostel and threw themselves down on just-vacated beds.

Clarence's mind invariably whirled around like a dervish from one thought to another. Then, overcome by fatigue, he would fall asleep. No sooner did he shut his eyes than the wail of sirens announcing the next wave of bombers awakened him. Drained of every ounce of strength, with the bone-aching weariness of broken nights, he lived in a twilight zone, moving around in a trance. *Will I eventually look at the disintegrated bodies and become callous, uncaring?* he wondered.

He never got used to the fire or his thumping heart.

While bombs exploded, canteen workers served food in shelters. As time passed, relief committees organised library services and entertainments such as music and dancing in rest areas.

Clarence and Angus were relieved from ambulance work and posted to rest areas and underground shelter duties with Parry and Albert. 'I'm starting an amateur singing night,' Parry said. 'Care to join me?'

'Delighted,' Clarence replied. He loved to sing and knew that his Welsh friend had an excellent tenor voice.

Parry looked at Angus. 'We need a baritone.'

Angus smiled. 'You may count on me.'

'I'll join you as long as it doesn't clash with dancing nights,' Albert said. 'You should all come along too.'

'Done.' Parry spoke for the others, knowing they had been inseparable ever since their training at Manor House.

The singing classes were such a success that a member of the Entertainments National Service Association approached Parry to join the weekly concerts in twenty shelters. The dancing session proved a break from the mayhem outside too. Representatives from the newly formed Council for the Encouragement of Music and the Arts brought along gramophones and classical music recordings. Paper chains and decorations festooned shelter walls and folk danced, oblivious of the sound of bombing and anti-aircraft guns outside.

Clarence longed for Mary. If only she were here, dancing with him. He quelled the thought. Hopefully she was at home in Nottingham, safe from the constant strafing and bombing. Perhaps she had joined a sewing circle like some of the women in the shelters here. He prayed for her and his family.

The London Blitz continued until May 1941. Clarence counted back and realised that the horror had lasted for fifty-seven consecutive days.

CHAPTER 6

THE FAMILY

London, May 1941

The Blitz ended after one last raid in May 1941, when Hitler failed to crush the determination of the British and moved his bombers east to target Russia. The lull gave the population a chance to recover.

St Paul's Cathedral gazed down sorrowfully, yet serenely, at the ravaged ruins. Starlings whistled as they jostled for places to roost. The stars winked down on Londoners and once again, the city enjoyed peaceful nights.

The occasional bombing continued, but it was nothing compared to the Blitz. Clarence no longer dreaded moonlit raids, although he still had nightmares and cried out in fear. Vacant houses stared at him from once-curtained windows like empty eye sockets—their overgrown gardens strewn with wreckage. Homeless waifs wandered the ruins, pillaging anything of value. Once he stopped his vehicle to admonish them but they scooted off even before he could get out.

***

Meanwhile, back in Nottingham, Doug had enlisted in the army. After training for six weeks, he was posted to Surrey for the final brush-up of tactics, then sent home on embarkation leave. Eager to get to grips with the enemy, Doug wore his uniform with pride, but he missed his brother Clarence. Doug recalled that as a child, he used to stand on the railway lines with arms akimbo and play chicken as trains steamed towards him.

More than once, Clarence had dragged him off to safety. How well he remembered their trips to Skegness—the donkey rides on the beach, the rolling waves and ripples lapping the pebbled shores. When would he see his brother again?

Doug wished his friends and family a fond farewell and boarded the *Duchess of York*. The liner had been converted to a troopship, and the cabin fitted with new wooden bunks that looked like shallow coffins. They sailed via Durban in South Africa to avoid German submarines and raiders in the Mediterranean. The *Duchess of York* was at the head of a convoy, but destroyers constantly changed positions and either moved ahead or remained on the flanks. In the evenings, they winked their signals as if flirting with each other.

Rain fell in torrents and wind blew bursts of spray upon deck. The ship's stern rose and dipped in the heavy sea as they approached the Cape, but at Durban, the water was calm. Thousands of fairy lights trembled and danced in the town, reminding Doug of Skegness in peacetime.

They arrived in North Africa after a voyage of eight weeks and travelled by truck to Port Said. As they headed inland, flies landed on Doug's face and neck, making him regret his decision to enlist just a little. *To make things worse, the Nazis have ruined all our equipment, so we'll have to fire at Italian planes with pop guns*, he thought.

Several lorries waited for them at the docks. They were driven to base camp, and sent off for training in map reading and desert navigation—a difficult task in featureless sand or flat, stony areas. Doug was interested in vehicle maintenance, which, the sergeant said, would prove useful in the months to follow.

After six weeks of training, the men received a few days' leave to visit Cairo.

The women in black veils and Bedouins in white flowing robes fascinated Doug. Refugees from Europe thronged the streets. People considered Egypt a safe refuge, so thousands whom had managed to escape from the Nazis had gathered here. The city had an illusion of gaiety, despite the grumble of the guns a hundred miles off to the west.

They drove to the pyramids in a horse-drawn gharry. Doug stood in awe beside the stone blocks, each taller than a man. One of his mates, a Welsh tenor, entertained them with excerpts from Aida as they climbed the pyramid steps.

Later on, he rode on a camel. An amazing experience! So unlike riding a horse.

At King Farouk's Palace, belly dancers moved around the arena, contorting their bodies. Someone whispered to watch her navel wink, and Doug could hardly control his laughter.

Cairo was only half-blacked-out. The streetlights were painted blue, but houses and shops remained free from restrictions. Sunset brought one of the most beautiful scenes he'd ever witnessed. At twilight, the sky took on a purple tinge and stars appeared, and trees gave out a heavenly perfume.

Back at base camp, Doug couldn't sleep at nights because of the low growl of the RAF heading towards enemy lines. The men were under the command of Major General Richard O'Connor, but General Wavell was Commander-in-Chief of all the land forces.

Doug looked forward to seeing some action at last! He had enlisted to fight for king and country, not to sit in his tent and swat flies. Doug found the heat intolerable as the winds were as hot as a gust from a ship's engine room.

The men had a few days' leave at Alexandria, where they stayed at a boarding house. As they drove through the town, native children begged for biscuits, bully beef and baksheesh. The streets were crowded with dogs, beggars and shoeshine boys. Barrage balloons floated overhead.

Despite this, Alexandria seemed utterly remote from the world of war—cosmopolitan and cheerful with its hot baths and ice-cold drinks.

On Doug's return from leave, he was stationed at a place so full of flies that he swallowed the pests whenever he opened his mouth to speak or to eat. Scorpion baiting was now his only sport. He found one, put a ring of petrol around it and set the fuel alight. It stung itself to death rather than face the flames.

As the weather grew hotter, the men handed back their battle-serge and changed into khaki-drill. Because of the scarcity of water, they received only one gallon a day.

Doug longed to consume glass after glass of fresh water.

***

In July, Clarence received an envelope postmarked Durban. Eyes misted from tears, he paused to wipe his glasses. He pictured Doug, his light brown curls waving in the breeze. He clenched his fist, knowing his brother would soon face the horrors of war.

After perusing the letter, Clarence straightened his shoulders as if to relieve the pressure of his thought, glanced at his watch, and headed for the dining room. The smell of toast reached him even before he entered the mess room.

Angus had reserved a place for him at their table, and with a jerk of his head, he signalled Clarence to take the empty seat beside him. His huge hand dwarfed the spoon he held above a bowl of steaming porridge.

'We had a ruckus at the Savoy,' Albert was saying. 'The communists arranged a rally just outside the hotel and were encouraging East Enders to demand admittance into the air raid shelter for patrons.'

Clarence dropped himself into the chair. 'Were they allowed in?'

Parry dipped a piece of toast into a plate of bubble and squeak. 'Management had to let them in,' he said, before taking a bite.

Angus laughed. 'Did they settle down for the night?'

'The intruders were absolutely awed at the grandeur,' Albert answered. 'They stared at the chandeliers in silence and left when the all-clear sounded. At the next siren, police stood by, ready to escort them elsewhere. They followed, leaving the splendour of the Savoy for the squalid, smelly shelter near their homes.'

Clarence stifled a yawn. 'Communists stirred them up because they're against war with Germany.'

Albert rose to his feet and rubbed his eyes. 'During raids, wealthy West Enders visit air raid shelters in poverty-stricken East End.'

'Odd form of amusement,' Parry said.

Angus stretched his arms upwards, nearly hitting the cardboard lampshade that had been placed over the naked electric bulb for the blackouts at nights. 'Aren't they afraid of catching lice or scabies? The stench is sickening.'

'They hold perfumed hankies to their noses, and take a glimpse to satisfy their curiosity,' Albert said. 'Pity they don't pitch in and help them.'

Clarence yawned. His legs felt like lead. 'I'm sure they will. They were probably trying to find out if they could do anything.'

The friends staggered up the stairs, ready for bed after their night shift.

Towards the end of 1941, when a lull in the bombing ensued, ending the worst of the emergency in London, Clarence and Angus had weekends off from ambulance duties. They spent their Saturday evenings relaxing at a cinema or club. The Sugar Loaf and The Old Mahogany Bar became familiar locations.

'I've booked four tickets at the Windmill Theatre. Thought we needed a change,' Angus said one morning at breakfast in the hostel.

'How much do I owe you?' Clarence asked.

Angus hesitated. 'I ought to warn you. Nude ladies will be on stage, but they're in a tableau like a Raphael or Michelangelo painting.'

'You're pulling my leg.'

Angus shook his head. 'Albert and Parry are going too. It's a beautiful show. Nothing crude, I assure you. Come on. You can look away if there is a bawdy scene.'

Clarence hesitated, not wanting to place his morals in jeopardy. 'I think I'll remain here and write some letters. It's degrading for the women to expose their bodies. They only lead men into sin.'

Before leaving, they waved to him. Angus sauntered along and Parry lumbered off. Albert's stately carriage reminded Clarence how unlike the four of them were. Like Alexander Dumas's *The Three Musketeers*, their motto had been *all for one and one for all*. How long would they be together? Was he being too rigid, too sanctimonious?

His friends departed, laughing and joking among themselves. Their laughter melted his resolve, and he found the temptation to be with his chums irresistible. He loved their company and resolved to look away if the scene was obscene.

Clarence puckered his lips and let out a long low whistle.

As one, they stopped and turned. 'Cheerio, chum. We'll be seeing you,' Angus called out.

Clarence cupped his hands to his mouth. 'Do you still have that ticket?'

'In my pocket.'

'Don't need to dress up. Anything will do,' Parry said.

He raced back with Angus. Parry linked his arm through Clarence's while Angus took the other. They practically dragged him from his chair. Albert stood, gazing at the contrasting figures of his three friends. The show was beautiful with the lighting. There had been no bawdy laughter or rude jokes from the audience—only sighs of appreciation for the beauty displayed on stage. Clarence flushed with pleasure, and thought of Mary back home.

As the need for the Ambulance Unit in London decreased, one person after another left for service overseas. At the Old Mahogany Bar, Clarence, Angus, Parry and Albert discussed the pros and cons of volunteering abroad. A picture of the king and queen occupied a prominent position on a wall. Wisps of smoke rose to Toby mugs on the shelf above, and drifted towards the ceiling, now stained yellow with nicotine. Someone thumped out *Lillie Marlene* on the piano.

Parry was the first to decide. 'Going to China.'

'I'm sure they need assistance,' Angus agreed, 'but I'm wondering about India. The Japs have driven us out of Burma and may invade India any day. We'll be busy looking after the wounded.'

Albert nodded. 'Yes. Thousands of our boys have trekked over the Himalayas from Burma. They're suffering from dysentery, cholera or malaria. Refugees from Burma need help too.'

He glanced at Clarence. 'What about you, chum?'

'I'm still thinking it through, but the Far East is high on my list. Like Parry, I've been considering volunteering for work there. China has been at war longer than any other country and has suffered a lot. I long to help where the need is greatest.'

Angus slapped him on the back. 'Trust you to volunteer for the most difficult job.'

Early in December, casualties from North Africa streamed into London's Victoria Station. A member of the FAU, who had escorted the wounded, brought Clarence a letter from Doug. He retired to his room at the hostel and sank down on the bunk as thoughts of his brother flooded him with worry. He gazed out of the window at the icicles hanging from the bare branches of trees. The frozen droplets hung on until the sunlight thawed them. *Like mankind clinging to life after two and a half years of war,* Clarence thought.

Was it necessary to remain in England now the Blitz had eased? Should he volunteer for ambulance duties in Africa or China? He debated whether he'd choose Cairo, simply to be near Doug. The need for volunteers in China was greater, and the dangers from bombs and sickness far more likely than in Egypt. Civilians were under attack by the Japanese—the women were raped and people routed out of their towns and villages.

The tug-of-war between volunteering for North Africa or the Far East wrenched him in both directions, tearing him apart. At times, anger against the enemy overcame Clarence and he clenched his fists. He wanted to hit back with the bayonet, the gun or the grenade. His passion surprised him. *Is there a killer within me, lying dormant, only to come to the surface now? Was I wrong to register as a conscientious objector? Perhaps I should enlist in the army after all.*

He fingered the leather binding of his Bible, recalling his hatred of war and revulsion of killing. Worn down by doubts, Clarence lay back biting his lips.

The exquisite refrain of a nightingale broke the stillness. Spellbound, he listened to the sublime notes rising and falling. It was not every day that he heard one. Most of London's birds had died or deserted the city during the Blitz, so their singing was even rarer than in pre-war times.

He considered the birdsong to be the voice of a messenger from heaven because it came to him at the precise moment he had commenced his nightly prayers. The impulse to help the Chinese swelled within him, growing stronger until it proved irresistible, sweeping away all indecision. *I have received my answer. God has sent His creature to show me the way.*

Next morning, the FAU posted a list on the information board, asking for volunteers to China. Clarence grabbed his pen and placed his name at the top.

The sixteen months since the Blitz had ended seemed like a dream to Clarence. Apart from a few get-togethers with his friends, he was given a week's home leave every four months. At times he was also sent to the London FAU Office to relieve office staff who were given time off from their duties. The following year, in September, Clarence obtained leave to attend Eva's wedding.

The train for Nottingham was packed, but even more people squeezed into the carriage. The blacked-out windows threw a dark veil over everything, and he couldn't see clearly. He fumbled to get his dried egg sandwiches from his bag and took a bite. His stomach lurched at the taste. Like sawdust. He thought of the delicious buttered slices with freshly-laid eggs that his mother used to make for him in the good old days, and swallowed hard.

He had finished eating when the siren sounded. The engine stopped at the nearest station to allow passengers to disembark and take shelter if they wished. The train then proceeded at the regulated twenty-five miles per hour, so as not to arrive at the next destination before the all-clear, in case it was bombed. Clarence remained seated, though aware of the danger from hit-and-run raids by solitary aircraft. After a while, he dozed off.

When the all-clear signal went, the train resumed its normal speed. It arrived late at Nottingham, and no one was on the platform to meet him. He stumbled in the dark, trying to find his way to the taxi rank, shuffling forward through the throng of people.

After some time, Clarence guessed he was on the pavement because he had to lift his feet a few inches before proceeding. *Where were the taxis?* A cloud passed over the stars, extinguishing what little light they had provided. The crowd had thinned out now, but he still heard the low mumble of voices and curses as people trod on each other's toes. He reached out, advancing at a slow pace.

Despite his precautions, he walked into what seemed to be a short, portly gentleman or lady. He stopped. 'I beg your pardon.'

A crash broke the silence. A man cursed and struck a match.

'Put that bloody light out,' a voice yelled.

The flame was extinguished, but in those brief seconds Clarence recognised he was apologising to a pillar box. He grinned with embarrassment.

The cloud lifted. Only a few yards away, taxis were lined up and he took one home.

Twenty minutes later, he was back at Carlton, Nottingham, holding his mother in his arms. It was cold and dark when he got there, but the warm caresses and cosy fireside spread a glow of happiness over him.

Albert and Eva were married the next day at the Netherfield Baptist Church. Eva looked radiant in white lace over a taffeta petticoat. Her hair hung loose and a coronet of orange blossoms surmounted an embroidered veil. She wore a pair of silver shoes and carried a bouquet of bronze-coloured chrysanthemums. The bridesmaid—Albert's younger sister, Winnie—was dressed in blue silk.

Despite his dislike of war, Clarence could not help admiring the groom, Albert Barker, who was in uniform and wore his cap at a rakish tilt.

The organ boomed out the *Wedding March* as the newlyweds walked down the aisle. The ceremony was beautiful, and his heart clenched as he thought of Mary. Had he spoken to her, perhaps they, too, would be walking down the aisle.

Watson and Ada held the reception at their home. Useful gifts like food parcels or cakes of soap lay displayed on a table. Fifty guests were present, but Clarence missed Doug, who was serving in the Royal Army Service Corps.

His brows rose in disbelief at the sight of a grand three-tiered wedding cake.

Roy slid up to him and whispered, 'There's only a homemade sponge below. The rest is all cardboard. Mum borrowed it from the baker.'

When the time came to cut the cake, Eva took off the top to reveal a small chocolate covered one underneath. The guests pretended not to notice. Glad that Roy had warned him about it, Clarence showed no surprise.

Albert had smuggled some whiskey back from Wales. Watson drank a toast to the young couple, and Clarence toasted the wedded pair with reconstituted orange juice. He appraised his sister, relieved she'd finally settled down and married. *What would the future bring her,* he wondered. *If her husband died in the war, she'd be like countless other widows without any future …*

His thoughts turned to Mary once again. He'd refrained from declaring his love for her as that would rush them both headlong into a marriage, which might only last a few months. He had no desire to leave her a widow should he lose his life during the Blitz.

After Albert and Eva left for their honeymoon in Wales, someone sang *White Christmas* and everyone joined in. The reception ended when Watson Dover started to sing *We'll Meet Again*. His powerful baritone voice thundered above the sound of his wife's subdued sobs.

The next morning, before departing, Clarence with a lump in his throat gave his mother a lingering hug. Her eyes were wet with tears, probably at the thought of losing her daughter to another and her son to the war.

'Sorry, I had to be with the guests and didn't have enough time to talk,' she said.

'Don't worry, Mum. I'll soon be back.'

The family car was propped up on blocks in the garage because the petrol ration had run out, so Stan dropped Clarence off at the station on his motorcycle before leaving for work.

The train to London was packed, but Clarence was too immersed in his thoughts to bother about the discomfort or the dark interior. One thought remained dominant in his mind. Would he ever see his family again?

At St Pancras Station, the tall figure of Angus stood above the crowd on the platform. Clarence elbowed his way over to him.

'Welcome back,' Angus said. 'How was the wedding?'

'Grander than I expected under the circumstances.' Clarence jerked his head towards wagonloads of rubble. 'Do they intend to dump that lot in the ocean?'

'Nothing gets wasted these days,' Angus replied. 'The debris from bombed buildings will go to the south-west to build runways for our airfields.'

Clarence couldn't help thinking how many missing body parts and precious items were among the fragments. He shuddered. On his return to the hostel, Clarence found a letter from Parry waiting for him. His friend had left for China with five others from his team.

Parry departed in the cargo ship *City of Venice* from the P & O Line. They had stopped for three weeks at Durban, South Africa and then continued sailing until they reached Bombay. There, they disembarked and travelled by rail to Calcutta, where they remained for a week.

At Dibrugarh, Parry stayed at the Assam Club. He had been having a great time until an attack of malaria confined him for weeks in hospital with the shakes.

Clarence read the letter and thumped his fist on the table. He walked up and down in his room like a caged animal, clenching and unclenching his fists. When would he be able to join them?

Ashamed at his outburst, he slouched into his chair and put his hands before his face for a few minutes. After a while he rose and paced the room, clasping his hands behind his back. He must be patient. Everything would turn out right in the end.

Four long months passed before his prayers to work in China were answered. Clarence was given embarkation leave before his departure. He thought of his last meeting with Mary when she had left him in a huff. He cast her words over in his mind, assessing the tone of voice she'd used, recalling the expression on her face and the movement of her head as she turned away.

Before leaving London, Clarence gripped his pen and wrote to Mary, informing her of his imminent departure and asking if he could meet her before he left.

No one was at Nottingham Station to greet him, so he hailed a taxi, impatient to get home.

When alone with his mother, he asked, 'Does Eva still live here?'

'Yes. Houses are scarce and it's safer for her to remain here. She's happy now and enjoys more independence since her marriage.'

Eva drifted into the kitchen and joined them. She picked up a little wicker basket filled with eggs and glanced at Clarence. 'Look. Fresh eggs. Albert often sends us half a dozen of them from Wales.'

He noted her lips curling up in a sneer and knew she considered him a coward for not enlisting in the army. Only his mother and Doug, who was a happy-go-lucky fellow, understood him. *Pity Doug wasn't here now.*

He strode over to Roy and tousled his hair. 'Do you still dream of being a messenger boy?'

The lad drew back his head and threw it like a horse tossing its mane. Clarence knew his youngest brother planned to enlist as soon as he turned eighteen if the war lasted long enough. *How many of us will be together when peace returns?* Deep in thought, he sub-consciously pinched the skin at his throat and wrinkled his brow.

A few days before his departure from Nottingham, Clarence met Mary at church. She wore a blue dress, which reflected the colour of her eyes. She smiled at him as he entered. He longed to sit beside her but slipped into the seat behind, just as he used to before their introduction. Once again, her elusive perfume stirred him and his heart beat rapidly.

After the service, Clarence strode up to her, more confident now. She held out her right hand and he grasped it. Mary put her left palm over his and squeezed it.

They gazed into each other's eyes, then wordlessly, they walked hand in hand towards the Abbey Gardens. Hawthorn hedges were smothered in creamy white blossoms. A robin trilled and a blackbird sang full-throated in a tree.

He led her to a quiet spot in the garden. 'Oh Mary,' he started to say but she placed her finger to his lips.

'Let's make the most of our time together. There's a dance on at the Parish Hall tonight.'

He could hardly contain his excitement. His voice sounded husky with emotion. 'I would like that.'

Clarence wore khaki as he longed for Mary to see him in uniform. Besides, he didn't want to face hostile gazes on his last day.

Her eyes lit up with pleasure when they met. He flushed. *Our previous quarrel has only served to draw us closer.*

Far into the night, until the hall closed, they waltzed to the hit tunes of the time. They agreed to walk home to talk things over, rather than take the bus. He slid his arm around her waist. Feeling the motion of her body as she walked, his pulse raced and he grew hot. She stopped and laid her head on his chest while he nuzzled her neck and breathed in her fragrance. His heart carried him away. 'What can we do but trust in the Lord?' he said.

He lingered outside the front door of Mary's house. Not wishing to prolong the agony of parting, however, he did not go indoors. Before leaving, he gathered her into his arms and kissed her as passionately as he dared. She returned his embrace.

Overcome by emotion, he turned and strode off without glancing back.

CHAPTER 7

A WARTIME VOYAGE

Liverpool, November 1942

On Saturday 7 November 1942, Clarence received orders to board the *SS Strategist* at Liverpool, and a lorry pulled up at Philpot Street to take the FAU volunteers to the docks. Clarence swung up into the vehicle and sat musing on the wooden bench as they wound their way north. What a hectic time he'd been through. The pressure. Always something to do. Who would have believed he could cope with the Blitz? He thought he'd never have the strength to deal with the fires but with God's grace he'd come through.

The lorry pulled up at Princess Quay. The white upper decks and blue bands on the *SS Strategist's* funnels had been painted over in battleship-grey. The ship was part of a convoy that consisted of tramp steamers and empty tankers—the latter to return with oil.

Fifty-four passengers, including men from the FAU and soldiers from the regular army, lined up on the wharf. When ordered to board the ship, they moved forward and mounted the gangplank. Clarence expected to breathe in the salty flavour of the ocean and hear the swell of waves, but instead, the odour of grease and fresh paint greeted him. The constant hum of motors drummed on his ears.

The crew checked their boarding cards, briefed them on how to act during an emergency, assigned each person to a lifeboat, and conducted passengers to their cabins. Clarence shared one with Albert, Angus, Stephen and two others he hadn't met. Bill Skurr, who was in charge of the China party, had a separate cabin. He was a Quaker, good-looking with a youthful face. Clarence had worked with his brother Jack in London, during the Blitz.

An electric fan whirred in its guarded bracket. Six bunks and a metal storage locker filled the small cabin. Clarence dumped his gear on a bunk and set about tidying his things. He spent the next couple of days exploring the ship and getting to know his roommates. On the third day after boarding, a dull throbbing arose below decks. Dockworkers dropped hawsers into the dark waters of the Mersey, severing the umbilical cord to home. The ship steamed off, its wake growing in width as momentum increased. It left the estuary and veered north towards the open sea.

The friends braved the ice-cold wind on deck, and watched as the shores of their homeland slipped away—perhaps for the last time. A thudding sound from deep below indicated an increase in the ship's heartbeat. Beckoned by a distant lighthouse, the convoy passed to the west of the Isle of Man.

Clarence had never left England. The thought of travelling to the Far East had thrilled him, but now icy fingers clutched at his throat. A faint whiff of coal reminded him of his childhood days when the family lived near a railway siding at Netherfield. His thoughts floated back on the crest of the waves to Mary. The slow slapping of the sea against the ship's side became a waltz measure. In his mind's eye, he held her in his arms as they danced to its rhythm.

They were a good team, both endowed with the love of God. A swell of emotion rose within him. Only a few days ago he'd been with her, and now a vast expanse of water divided them.

The sea changed to a steely grey and a squall arose. *SS Strategist* nose-dived into the oncoming waves as they negotiated the Irish Sea. Clarence held his breath as the ocean surged, spraying his clothes. Soon the old tramp turned west—away from Scotland—to cross the Atlantic. A current of air tumbled in, fluttering the flags at the masthead and carrying off the blue-grey smoke from its funnels.

The ship rolled and shuddered, steaming through mountains of water. Snow-capped peaks slammed against the hull, raising *SS Strategist* in the swell.

Clarence stood on deck, leaning on the rail and looked down at the foredeck where the bosun had men at work. Nearby, a passenger lost his footing and slid across the deck, stopping only when he hung onto someone's legs. He scrambled to his feet, looking sorry for himself.

Clarence clutched the ship's railing. His stomach heaved. In the next few moments everything was compressed into a fast-moving sequence as in a nightmare. He turned ashen grey, leaned over and spewed. The wind blew the vomit back on him, leaving a slimy mass on his clothes.

He staggered to his cabin with a sour taste in his mouth and a sickening stench from his shirt. His companions were already lying on their bunks, drenched in sweat.

The ship's doctor distributed tablets, but nothing helped.

Five days out of Liverpool, on Friday 13 November, the squall started to abate and Clarence staggered to the dining room on unsteady legs. After breakfast, he hastened to the middle deck where the fresh breeze was a welcome relief from the stagnant air below.

It grew colder, and on the horizon, the sea and sky embraced. Clarence went back to his cabin for his greatcoat and a scarf his mother had knitted. He fondled it, imagining his mother's fingers flying as she worked through the wool, weaving a prayer for him into each stitch.

He searched for a more sheltered spot and tucked his hands deep in his pockets. Rugged up as he was, the Atlantic wind penetrated his bones, piercing his ears like a sharp knife. Here, ships had to contend not only with the ferocity of the ocean, but also the severe cold, and their underwater foe—the submarine.

Through the haze, Clarence caught glimpses of the escort. Flying boats, big and slow Sunderlands, droned around at odd intervals throughout the day. One flew low, throwing curtains of spray on either side of its fuselage and landed with a deafening thud.

When the sun dipped below the horizon, the bosun piped a shrill whistle, giving the order to darken ship. The crew then shut portholes and dampened down the fire in the galley. The smallest chink of light could betray their presence to an enemy trained to look for a crack in the armour, or a door left ajar. If any gleam showed—whether steaming lights or even a lighted cigarette—the corvettes would heave to and call out.

Angus took out a cigarette, put it to his lips and was about to light it.

Clarence laid a restraining hand on his arm. 'You know I object to smoking and can't tolerate it in our cabin, chum. Sorry, but you'll have to find somewhere else to smoke.'

Angus glared at his friend and shook off his hand, but he left, banging the door shut on his way out. He stamped off on deck to enjoy a quiet fag.

Soon a corvette drew aside and someone called out over the hailer. 'Put that bloody light out!'

Angus stubbed out his cigarette and swore, before heading for the toilet.

That night as Clarence lay in his cabin, his thoughts returned to his family. How many of them would survive the war? What was Mary doing now? Did she think of him as frequently as he did of her? Would she still love him by the time hostilities were over? He knew his love for her would never change.

He fell asleep thinking of her.

The next night, Clarence walked outside on the deck, watching the clouds scurry across the horizon. The moon shed its radiance, its lights refracting rainbows through the spray. *Was Mary looking at the same bright luminary?* He longed to tell her of his travels. He blew a kiss, hoping it would reach her, then checked if anyone had seen him, but he was alone on deck. He decided to return to his cabin and met a stream of people in their lifejackets on the stairways. Alarm bells shrieked and the tide of humans forced him back.

'Get to your bloody boat station, mate,' someone shouted.

Clouds had gathered in the sky, blotting out the moon. Unsteady with the incessant swaying, Clarence stumbled in the dark towards his assigned lifeboat, clinging to the handrail.

The crew was trying to manoeuvre the boat into the correct position.

Corvettes made sweep after sweep of the ocean, dropping depth charges. Like a giant sledgehammer, each explosion sent tremors through the ship. The waves struck the keel, sending vibrations skimming along the deck and up the superstructure. The sea erupted, dispatching tons of water into a vertical jet, then fell back, unable to stand at attention any longer. It simmered down, but no debris floated up to the surface.

The submarine had escaped.

Clarence remained glued to the spot. *Was this to be their tomb?* Fear locked his legs. He scarcely dared breathe. *This is what war did to a man— turned his limbs to water and made his tongue as dry as sandpaper. In London, I'd been able to do something to help, but now I am powerless to aid others or myself.*

The night grew cooler. Turning up the collar of his greatcoat, Clarence dug his hands deep into his pockets. Time dragged until the captain gave orders for the passengers to return to their cabins.

Clarence fumbled his way back to his bunk, flung himself down on the bed and turned over to his chums. 'Good night.'

Loud snores told him they had already wandered to the field of unconsciousness.

The next morning, Albert roused them and pointed to a far-off light. 'Look! Bodies and debris! A torpedo has hit one of our ships.'

'Where?' a chorus of voices sang out.

'Just focus on the halo of oil.'

Clarence gasped, 'What a way to die.'

'The bloody U-boat was waiting for us,' Angus exclaimed.

Albert reached out for the railing for support. 'Poor chaps. They're flotsam now.'

The sight of the wreck mesmerised Clarence. It was too far off to see clearly, but, in his mind's eye, he visualised the floating corpses, now black and bloated.

SS Strategist steamed ahead without stopping to search for survivors. Clarence fisted his hands into two tight balls. It had never occurred to him that fellow men would be left to their fate. How heartless it seemed. If he'd been in their place, he'd have felt betrayed.

He controlled his feelings and thought logically. A stationary ship was an easy target for the enemy. He realised the importance of sacrificing the lives of a few survivors, who may only live for a few days after swallowing so much engine oil. *It was imperative to save a whole shipload of passengers and their essential cargo.*

They were out of range of U-boats by mid-November, so the escort wished them happy steaming before heading back to Liverpool. Then *SS Strategist* and a dozen ships sped along in single file. Ship after ship split from the line and headed for their homeport, leaving them alone.

Despite being out of range of the U-boats, the threat of an enemy raider or aircraft still remained. A blanket of silence fell on everyone. Each feared the worst. Clarence's sense of helplessness screamed a warning in his mind, bringing home the meaning of the word *pacifist*: peace-lover, peacekeeper, conscientious objector, anti-war, anti-violence. *What did it mean to be one now? To be helpless, powerless, vulnerable.*

Clarence gazed at the ship's twelve-pounders and longed to protect the convoy from Nazi U-boats. His hands itched to grab the guns and fire into the depths at their enemy but he could not bring himself to do that because of his beliefs.

Before an hour had passed, Bill Skurr announced, 'The Second Officer wants all able-bodied civilians to assemble in the dining room prior to afternoon tea.'

The news spread rapidly and the non-combatants gathered in silence.

The officer, a young man who was not much older than Clarence, waited until the passengers had assembled. 'I need assistance,' he said. 'The crew is on night duty. Could you pitch in and help with lookout duties during daylight hours? Search for anything at odds with the normal. It won't involve any shooting.

'An officer will post a roster on the notice board. I know I may rely on your co-operation.' He used diplomatic skill, and avoided the word *conscientious objectors*, eliciting a unanimous response.

On the way back to their cabin, Bill said, 'If a raider or a U-boat launches an attack at us, I've no idea what can be done.'

'It's a case of playing cat-and-the-mouse,' Clarence replied. 'Scamper off before the enemy sees you. Slip beyond the horizon and elude him.'

'Yes. Cat and mouse: *house*, as our cockney lads at home would say,' Albert quipped, recalling London's East Enders.

Clarence shrugged. 'I never could understand their way of speaking.'

Regardless of whether U-boats were around or not, it was necessary to maintain watch. The crew showed the strain on their faces and dark rings formed under their eyes. The captain remained on the bridge at critical times. Clarence had presumed he did the steering, but the helmsman, who held the rank of quartermaster, steered the ship and took his orders from whoever was on duty at the time.

Bill made friends with one of the officers. 'May we have a look at the bridge?' he asked.

'I'll mention your request and get back to you,' the officer answered, before walking off with a lurching gait so typical of seamen.

Clarence thought he had forgotten about them, but a few days later when the weather was calm, the captain invited Bill and his friends over.

The constant chatter from the radio room and throb of the engines sounded above the roar of the waves. The helm was quite small, no bigger than the steering wheel of a car. The polish on the teak floors of the bridge left a pleasing odour and a mirror-like sheen.

'I challenge the most meticulous housewife to keep her house as spick and span as this,' Angus said.

Clarence smiled. His own mother would be ready to take up the challenge any day. His chest heaved at the thought of his house-proud mum.

Luckily, the days grew warmer as they steamed towards the tropics. Passengers unpacked their tropical kit and changed into lighter clothing. Clarence's lips parted and he sucked in a deep breath at the sight of a crimson sunset on one side, and a silvery moon on the other. Darkness swiftly followed half an hour of twilight. He missed the long summer evenings of home.

The convoy had taken a round-about route to India in order to avoid enemy U-boats, and headed for South America with the intention of heading to South Africa later. Clarence hoped to reach Cape Town or Durban in time for Christmas.

The wind grew in strength and gigantic clouds towered above. Like a hysterical housewife, a storm rocked the ship, smashing the glassware. Clarence and Albert were on duty at the time. They hung onto the rails, while the men below wedged themselves into a corner.

Next day, the wind eased, but waves continued to break on the lower decks. Clarence joined the others on the focsle, which provided a haven from the exposed lookout areas. He lowered his body into a deck chair in the sun and let its warmth thaw him out. After a few minutes, he attempted a conversation but they were half asleep, and he found himself conducting a monologue. He watched the waves, letting his mind drift into the sanctuary of secret thoughts and longings.

Within an hour, a wave swept over the deck, drenching their clothes and breaking sleep from its moorings. Angus leapt to his feet, swearing. He scurried for the hatchway leading to their cabins—the tattoo of the naked girl on his arm embracing him like a mermaid.

Later on, the sea took on a mirror-like appearance and left everyone in good spirits as they steamed south. Flying fish skimmed along, then dropped back and surfed on the bow wave. Sunbeams danced across the white caps. Someone sang *On the Road to Mandalay*, and all joined in, showing a bold front to fear.

On Thursday 26 November, rumours reached them that a torpedo had hit one of the ships, so the *SS Strategist* took evasive action and changed course, sailing east for part of the day.

Just before midnight, they sighted a rainbow-coloured ring reflecting like fairy lights in the moonlight. Debris floated on the water. Clarence eased his collar. He choked to think that amid the debris were corpses of men who'd been alive just a few hours ago. 'That could easily have been us,' he said.

The wreck remained in view for half an hour before vanishing.

In the morning, Clarence saw another wrecked ship on the starboard. Shading his eyes with one hand, he pointed with the other. 'It appears to be bow down and makes no smoke.' He wiped his tears. 'Poor devils. Most of them were boys. Just eighteen years and a bit over.' He felt quite mature at twenty-three.

Such a waste! Had their dying brought the war any closer to an end? No, it was probably a mere drop in the ocean. He clenched his fists and bit his lip. His fingernails dug into his flesh and drew blood.

CHAPTER 8

CHRISTMASTIDE

On board the SS Strategist, December 1942

SS Strategist zigzagged its way across the Atlantic, heading for Brazil. By the second day of December, passengers sighted Olinda harbour, and thronged to the rails, eager to set foot on *terra firma*. Known as the *Venice of Brazil*, Recife, the capital of Pernambuco, nosed the Atlantic Ocean just south of the equator. The city stood only four miles south of the entrance to the port.

Dozens of small fishing boats and several American and Brazilian warships had anchored inside the breakwater. The crew milled about on deck, some dressed as if they were on shore leave.

The pilot's motor boat tossed about in the sea as it fought its way towards them. When the craft chugged in beside the ship, two crewmen threw out a Jacob's ladder that clattered against the side as the pilot hauled himself up. He looked like a comic opera sea captain with his black moustache curled upwards, but he took the vessel into harbour for a well-earned rest from her travails.

Three hours after docking at Recife, Clarence and a batch of passengers were taken ashore. The river cut its way through the metropolis and majestic palms on the riverbanks waved a welcome. Shops stocked food, clothing and watches. Boys laden with oranges, mangoes, razor blades, toffee and other little necessities crowded around.

'Hello, Jack. Want to buy?' they called out, their white teeth flashing in the sunlight.

The FAU ignored the throng of sellers and took a couple of taxis to the Palace Hotel. Taxis and limousines flying diplomatic ensigns had the roads to themselves as the government had requisitioned all private vehicles. Most people travelled by tram, which was always packed. The conductor balanced like a trapeze artist on the step outside the carriage, while checking tickets.

Children played hopscotch on the black and white mosaic pavements. Locals stood on their doorsteps, enjoying the sea breeze; others sat smoking at café tables. They spoke in Portuguese. The language sounded strange to Clarence's ears—exotic and puzzling at the same time.

At the hotel, he met some English merchant naval crew. After chatting for a while, one of the men shared their story, 'Our ship was torpedoed off Dakar by an Italian submarine, and we've been living here for a week now. We'll be leaving by air for New York and travelling back to England by ship. Any letters for the family?'

Clarence rubbed his hands. 'I've some mail for my mother. I'd appreciate it if you could post them in England for me.'

'Delighted.'

Racing up to his room two steps at a time, Clarence returned with two stamped and sealed envelopes—one for his mother and another for Mary. *They should reach them by Christmas.*

Later on when they had unpacked, Clarence and three of his friends took the tram to Olinda, about four or five miles from Recife, where a battery of four guns had their sights trained on the harbour. The friends wandered down to the sea and upon finding some bathing huts, changed and raced across the sands for a swim. The smooth sand was so unlike the pebbly beaches of England.

Unable to bear the blistering sun and the burning sand, they flung themselves into the water. Once in, Angus started a water fight and they all teamed up with a partner, releasing their pent up emotions and letting their fears of being torpedoed slide off their shoulders with the jets of water from each other.

Exhausted, they collapsed in a heap, laughing like school boys at a picnic.

Breakfast usually consisted of fruit and bread rolls with lots of butter. At lunch and dinner, they had soup, fish, chicken or steak and macaroni. Clarence salivated at the aroma of spices and the sight of a well-laden table. He devoured his steak and mushroom sauce with relish. Dessert was pineapple, bananas and oranges.

After so long on rations, his thoughts dwelt on nourishment. *Strange that people can satisfy their appetites on the opposite side of the globe while Europe starves. If only some of the food arrives safely in England for the war-torn country.*

A brisk walk brought them to the caged leopards and cheetahs. After watching them being fed, the odour of animal urine and the deafening roars of the beasts drove them to seek the quiet of the refreshment room for a drink.

Lunch had been pre-ordered at the hotel so they returned for their meal before setting out to the British Country Club, hoping to get news of home. There they met some English ladies, who were only too eager to exchange news of England and recall old times.

Clarence relished the club's orangeade and twirled the glass in his hands, delighted to see the pips floating around. 'This is made from real oranges,' he said.

One of the ladies beamed. 'Whenever I hear of the rationing in England, I realise how fortunate we are over here.'

Angus rose from his seat. 'Please excuse us, ladies, but we must do some shopping while we get the chance.'

'Safe journey,' the women chorused, as the friends shook hands with them.

Before the ship's departure, Clarence bought a few handkerchiefs and a belt. Looking out to sea, they saw a British tramp limping in with a piece blown out of its bows. The ship was high in the water, as if cargo or ballast had been thrown overboard to lighten her.

Angus pointed to the jagged edges near the waterline. 'A close call!'

Clarence prayed for the Lord's continued protection during the rest of their voyage.

Three days later, they once again boarded the ship on Saturday 5 December and were under way within a couple of hours. The crew now commenced shooting practice, firing the four-inch stern gun first. A twelve-pounder released a smoke shell and four machine guns let off tracer bullets.

The smell of the gunpowder brought back images of Guy Fawkes Day. Like most boys, Clarence and his brothers had often played at being soldiers. He wandered over to watch the men in action. *Surely, a shot at an enemy is not wrong?*

One of the passengers, Henry, an army officer, who Clarence had met at dinner, stood watching the crew. Seeing Clarence approach, he moved over to him. 'It's good to get back at the enemy. I can't figure out how you fellows can dream of not fighting.'

Clarence rubbed his chin. 'It does worry me at times, but I can't bring myself to kill another man.'

Henry put his hands on his hips. 'How would you feel if the Nazis crossed the Channel and your mother or sister was in danger of rape? Would you grab a weapon to defend them or just look on and do nothing?'

Clarence clenched and unclenched his hands. 'Only the Lord knows how I'd act under such circumstances. Pacifists have been known to gun down enemies charging towards them while aiding the wounded on a battlefield. I've often wondered whether I'd do the same. How I'd act on the spur of the moment.'

'Then you should join the army and fight the foe.'

'No. Only God has the right to take away another's life. I've joined the FAU to help those who've suffered the consequences of war, but that is all my conscience allows me to do.'

'I think you pacifists use this excuse as a façade for cowardice. You hide behind the skirts of religion to conceal your fear of being killed!'

'I've heard this argument before,' Clarence replied, his face reddened. 'Perhaps some of us do, but many join the army to satisfy their blood lust. It's not always for king and country.' Clarence knew if he remained arguing, he'd only lose his temper and do something he'd regret. He turned on his heel and walked off.

Previously, the taunts of others had stiffened his views but now, among so many navy and army personnel, his stand for peace and against bloodshed weakened. How thrilling it would be to fight for king and country. *If I had joined the army like Doug, I'd now be in North Africa, fighting side by side with him.*

Clarence's will waned. He recalled that when the escort had fired depth charges on a German submarine, his mind had filled with dislike for the enemy lurking beneath, and he had searched hopefully for signs of its destruction.

The disturbing thoughts persisted, but he reassured himself he was doing God's will.

They accelerated southeast to Saldanha Bay. The weather grew cooler again and passengers resumed battle dress, discarding tropical gear. Albatross, with wing spans of up to five feet, dark brown on top but white underneath, glided on the crests of the waves. The birds followed in their wake until they reached Saldanha Bay.

A pilot came out in a red motorboat with a black 'P' on each bow and boarded the ship. Then he took them through the anti-submarine net and anchored the boat where four merchant ships huddled together, hidden from the sea by hills.

The captain went ashore to a military camp, but because it was a restricted area, both crew and passengers had to remain on board.

SS Strategist remained at anchor next to an American-built 'Victory' ship. It flew the red ensign, indicating that it had been registered in the UK. Clarence knew that the 'Victory' ships were built especially for the war, and took only sixty days to construct. The hulls were welded, instead of being held together by rivets but they were not as strong as them.

SS Strategist hugged the coastline for about sixty miles, and in three hours, the dim outline of Table Mountain appeared to rise out of the South Atlantic, dwarfing the lion-shaped Signal Hill. The city's signature landmark loomed into view against a background of piercing blue. Gulls wheeled above and screeched, while everyone vied for a spot on deck.

Clarence, Albert and Stephen remained on deck enjoying the view and watching the captain and an officer disembark, while Angus left to have a cigarette.

Stephen gazed at the mountain. 'Pity we're not allowed to get off. There's a cable car to the top.'

'It's a shame to visit Cape Town without going up to the top of Table Mountain,' Clarence agreed. 'Have you been here before?'

'Yes. The temperature plummets once you reach the summit.'

Clarence shuddered. They'd been in tropical seas only a few days ago and he had thawed out with the warmth. Although he would enjoy a trek up, the thought of being hit with cooler temperatures didn't appeal to him at that moment.

After dinner, everyone again crowded on deck to gaze at the massive slab of sandstone and quartz glimmering in the moonlight. The sky was clear and gave them a splendid vision. A little later, clouds rolled over Table Mountain's summit and long streaks of white mist appeared among the peaks of the distant mountains. A thin layer of fog, called the Tablecloth, shrouded the flat top.

By morning, amid dark clouds and a downpour of rain, they again became part of a convoy. A destroyer and a corvette escorted them. Most of the ships were laden with deck cargo, though some carried railway locomotives. It was all hush-hush about their destination, but that didn't stop everyone from speculating.

'As five of the vessels will not be stopping at Durban, I think they're off to the Middle East,' Clarence said. 'The engines are possibly for building the railway through Iran to Russia. She's now an ally, so everything we can spare from India is shipped across for them.'

The convoy followed the coastline. A few huts stood against a background of mountain ranges. The sea was calmer. Clarence stretched his legs out on deck, enjoying the view. He hoped to be in Durban for Christmas.

By Christmas Eve, a cool wind tempered the fierce heat of the sun. The mountains disappeared and a wooded shore unrolled in the mist. Occasionally three planes came in to reconnoitre but no enemy appeared. The escorting destroyer commenced firing practice. In the afternoon, an Avro Anson training plane flew up and down between the ships like a boy with a toy.

Christmas day was sunny but by evening, the weather turned windy and everyone fled to their cabins. Clarence missed the Christmas church service he used to attend back home with Mary. It was a pity that Quakers neither had a Christmas nor an Easter service. They only held services on Sundays, when the Friends gathered in Bill Skurr's cabin and sat silently. Participants contributed as the spirit moved them. Clarence loved those moments communing with God among his fellow men.

At dinner time, they hastened to the dining room. A menu informed them they would be enjoying hors-d'oeuvres, followed by tomato soup, and fish, turkey or ham served with green peas, kidney beans and potatoes. Dessert was plum pudding, mince pies and a pink and white iced cake.

Clarence shut his eyes, rejoicing in the Christmas cheer. He thought of his family back in England as his teeth sank into the roast. There'd be no turkey for them this Christmas.

During dessert, he wished he could send them a piece of the cake. He compared this festive cheer to the drab and cheerless Christmas of 1940, and a spurt of rage against Hitler filled him.

He quelled his anger with great effort and joined in the festivities.

Angus checked the bulletin board as they left the dining room. He pointed to a gaily-decorated programme pinned on the noticeboard. 'Must not miss the show.'

Albert pushed his way to the front and read the notice. 'An excerpt from Shakespeare's *A Midsummer Night's Dream*! That should be good.'

'Reminds me of our time at Stratford,' Clarence said.

After the concert, one of the crew handed out printed sheets of *White Christmas* as well as other carols. Another crewmember accompanied the singing on his harmonica. As they sang, Angus's voice vibrated more robustly than the rest.

The Empire broadcast and the king's speech ended the evening.

Clarence retired to his bunk at harmony with the world—all thoughts of fighting the enemy now subdued. *Christmas is a time of peace and goodwill. Hope the Nazis don't send their planes over to bomb dear Old Blighty tonight!*

On Boxing Day, *SS Strategist* and another ship, *Peshawar*, dropped anchor outside Durban harbour. In the daytime, the weather remained hot and sunny, but thunder and lightning shattered the night.

New Year's Day, greeted everyone with heavy rain. *SS Strategist* docked next to a Red Cross hospital ship. The crew changed into civilian clothes—identifying themselves by the silver letters 'MN' below a crown—as they were in a neutral port now.

Zulu women peddled strings of brightly-coloured beads and followed them, refusing to leave until they purchased something.

Clarence bought postcards to send home. He and his friends spent their time sightseeing, ambling along the waterfront, through the town and past the City Hall. Once they reached Marine Parade, the cool breeze wafted in from the Indian Ocean. The sound of children playing, the sun-tanned bodies and myriads of coloured beach brollies lulled them into a sense of peace.

'Really now! Is Durban unaware that there is a war?' Albert walked off while the others wandered over to a parlour and bought an ice cream cone.

Ten minutes later, he returned from a stroll around the shops, waving a map of Durban and its environs. 'Did you know that they have their own Midlands and a Nottingham Road? You should be at home here,' he called out.

Clarence took the map, chuckled and ran his finger over the familiar names.

Angus pointed to the place marked the Valley of a Thousand Hills. 'Let's go count them.'

Before the third gust of breeze blew in, they had caught a taxi.

The temperature dropped as they climbed high above the plain. Clarence breathed the clear air, glad to be away from his cabin. The driver stopped at a restaurant with a panorama over what *did* seem like a thousand hills. The town spread down from the peninsula to the harbour foreshore. 'Look at the beehive-shaped thatched huts,' Clarence exclaimed.

Charmed by the ambience and atmosphere of the restaurant, he ordered a fillet steak. It was cooked to perfection.

Before returning to the ship, they strolled to the shops and bought a few trinkets to send home as they were to depart the next morning.

Angus let his eyes wander over the vista unfolding before him. 'My, my. I could stay here forever.'

'Duty calls,' Clarence said. 'Time to report back.'

'Let's jump ship and remain behind,' Albert joked.

Clarence smiled. He'd rather be sharing the experience with Mary than his chums.

The ship was due to leave with a convoy of eleven ships and the hospital vessel *Oranje* on 6 January, but as many of the crew had deserted, the captain went in search of replacements. Before leaving, he trumpeted orders through the megaphone over the ship's creaking noises, announcing that everyone was to stand by for departure as he intended leaving port within a couple of hours.

'We returned promptly from the thousand hills only to be told to wait,' Albert grumbled.

Angus nodded. 'There was so much more we could have done.'

As the temperature grew hotter, so did tempers. Even at night, the cabins didn't lose their heat and the steel bulkheads remained warm.

On Saturday 9 January 1943, troop ships, escorted by corvettes, destroyers and cruisers, increased their velocity, leaving them behind since it was too dangerous to wait for lame ducks even in port.

When ready to depart, the *SS Strategist* sailed south-southeast on the vast expanse of ocean, solely in God's hands. The ship zigzagged all the way, taking evasive action to elude enemy submarines. Numb with fear, Clarence thought of the other British tramp that had a near miss. He clutched the handrail so tight that his fingers cramped. For nearly a fortnight, they passed only two ships in the lonely stretch of sea.

The heat increased as they approached the equator, which they crossed on 22 January. At Karachi, the ship went straight in and docked under the direction of the pilot. The capital of Sind was a busy port on a barren piece of land washed on three sides by the Arabian Sea. Male and female coolies toiled in the sun, unloading the deck cargo. Women with their colourful *saris* thrown gracefully over their shoulders moved fast and efficiently, their nose rings reflecting the sunlight.

'The men have no sense of chivalry,' Clarence said, with a flash of anger.

Angus shrugged. 'Native women are used to hard work. You can't teach them to change their ways.'

A sergeant met them at the docks and drove them to the Carlton Hotel, where they were to stay. Waiters served the meal with such style that they felt like kings.

Appetites satiated, they decided to go to the film *The Great Dictator*.

Bill haggled with the gharry *wallah* before getting in. 'How much?'

'Four *annas, sahib*.'

'One *anna*.' Bill half-turned to leave.

'No, *sahib*. Cinema is far. Three *annas*.'

At that moment, another horse-drawn carriage clomped up.

Bill was just about to hail it when the driver rocked his head from side to side. 'Come, *sahib*. For *you*, one *anna*.'

Clarence, Angus and Albert crowded into a gharry with Bill, intrigued by the four-seater light horse carriage that resembled a box.

'Cheaper than a taxi,' Bill said. 'In smaller towns they use two-wheeled horse-drawn carriages called pony carts.'

Back at the hotel, a message had arrived, giving orders to embark by train to Calcutta. Clarence gave a scarcely audible sigh, glad to have a taste of India before leaving for China.

At breakfast, he met some army officers with whom he had travelled on board *SS Strategist*. Henry, the officer who had argued with Clarence over pacifists, had been posted to the Burma front and the rest to the north-west frontier. He had a hunted look on his face. 'Japanese use Allied prisoners of war for bayonet practice,' he said to Clarence, the only person who paid him any attention.

The others were talking among themselves, their faces flushed with happiness. Secure in the belief they were safe from Japanese attack in India, they looked forward to being burra *sahibs* in the colonies.

Clarence shook hands with Henry. 'God be with you,' he said and meant every word.

Which of them would survive the war? His thoughts flew to Doug. He thought of the sand getting into his brother's eyes, the flies and scorpions. It made his flesh crawl. He visualised guns roaring, bombs falling and landmines exploding in the hot desert sands.

Recalling the Blitz and the sound of missiles plummeting to the earth, his stomach contracted into a tight ball. *Conditions in the Orient were probably even worse than back home. Soon I'll be there.* Clarence rubbed his hands in anticipation of doing his bit for war victims.

CHAPTER 9

A TRAIN JOURNEY

Karachi, January 1943

Clarence wished the soldiers, who had been his travelling companions on *SS Strategist*, the best of British luck and returned to the hotel to pack his things. In the warm predawn of the next morning, he had a shower. Refreshed, he towel-dried himself and changed. Folding his pyjamas, he placed them into his portmanteau, ready for the next leg of the journey.

The Friends Ambulance Unit found two compartments reserved for them at the station. Each compartment could hold four passengers and contained a private lavatory. Clarence shared a compartment with Albert, Angus and Stephen.

Stephen had spent some time in India. 'Watch out for the dirt and dust, flies and food, the heat, crowds and beggars,' he said.

On 31 January, 1943, the train commenced its long journey towards Calcutta and trundled across the flat, dry plains of north-western India.

The FAU had a fan and a bunk in their carriage but third-class passengers were lucky to secure a seat on a hard timber bench. Some sat on their luggage in the aisle or in the stinking toilets between carriages. Others rode on the footplates or sprawled on the roof of the carriage, where the evening air was cooler.

Stephen laughed. 'Don't worry about the sweat. It's the distinguishing mark of an Englishman in India. You'll soon get used to it.'

At night, Angus stretched out on the seats, while Albert and Stephen chose the overhead bunks that folded against the wall during the day.

Clarence stayed awake, jotting down notes and taking care not to knock his head on the bunk above him.

'Are you keeping a diary?' Stephen asked. 'I wish I could be as methodical as you.'

'This is a once-in-a-lifetime experience,' Clarence replied. 'Something to look back on. I may write a memoir one day.'

'Well. Good luck and good night.'

Dusk descended over the vast Indian plain as if someone had turned off a switch. Clarence opened the window, hoping to get some fresh air during the night.

'Shut the blasted window,' his companions groaned as a lungful of dust, smoke and soot greeted them.

Clarence lifted the catch and slid the wooden frame down.

The train hurtled across the Sind Desert, following the two rails that gleamed like silver ribbons in the moonlight. Clarence finished writing and put away his notes. The swaying of the carriage and the clicking sound of the rails relaxed his tired muscles. From his seat by the window, he stared, mesmerised by the sagging telegraph wires between each post. The flat, treeless plain stretched for miles. No sign of habitation greeted his gaze. A solitary camel left a trail of dust as it fled the iron monster. A boy urged his flock of goats along before disappearing beyond the horizon.

Within a half hour, the temperature dropped and the moon cast a silvery web over everything. A deep purple-blue sky caressed the land and hid beneath an ever darkening cape. A palm stood, silhouetted against the outline of a lonely village of low sand-coloured dwellings—the first Clarence had seen that evening.

He slipped his diary beneath his pillow and stretched himself out on the bench. His body rocked in rhythm with the clatter of the wheels on the expansion joints.

The train clanked to a halt at a station and the sound of shouting infiltrated the carriage around mid-day. A whole village seemed to have grown out of the desert.

A man carrying a yoke with a pot of hot tea suspended at one end and aluminium mugs on the other shouted, '*Char-wallah. Char-wallah,*' as he ran along the platform. A woman balanced a tray of fried vegetables battered in chickpeas and spices; another, grilled kebabs on an open fire. An aroma rose, titillating their taste buds.

Women cooked food on small braziers and travellers-in-transit camped at the station, making it their kitchen and bedroom. Cows wandered among inert bodies, nuzzling cabbages or bananas, but no one shooed them away as Hindus worshipped cattle.

All the while, passengers and railway officials picked their way around people stretched out on the bare floor. Food stalls lined the platform. Indian sweetmeats, fragrant rice and aromatic curries singed the air with their overpowering aromas. Clarence slackened his steps, amazed at a totally different culture from his own, little realising that within a short time, the smells, sights and sounds were to become commonplace to him.

He stopped before a stall selling Indian sweetmeats.

Stephen put his hand upon Clarence's shoulder. 'Come on. We must be careful what we eat. We don't want to get diarrhoea or dysentery.'

Although tempted to sample the delicious spread, Clarence restricted himself to buying oranges and bananas from which the bacteria-laden outer layer could be peeled off.

On their return to the carriage, like Mrs Havisham's room in the novel, *Great Expectations,* a coating of fine powder covered the floor. No matter how many times they wiped the benches, dust filtered through every opening.

The train rattled on as the four men chatted or gazed out of the window. The monotonous journey continued and another day waned.

Stephen took out his handkerchief and dabbed his face. 'In Bengali, the word twilight translates to cow-dust time because the fine sand is more noticeable then.'

Clarence gave a chuckle as he peered through the dust-covered window. The stories he heard about India were as colourful as the country itself, and as varied as the religious diversity of the people. 'Well, at least someone got it right. A boy in his bare feet and *dhoti* is driving a herd of cows, leaving a cloud of dust behind.'

Finally, darkness set in and the dim light bulb made it impossible to read. Clarence wiped away the dust, then lay down, his dreams filled with camels and Lawrence of Arabia.

At sunrise, the train stopped at another station to set down and pick up passengers. The attendant brought them breakfast of tea and toast, and placed their food down on the foldable tables. He remained with them until the next stop, where he alighted with the trays.

Clarence packed his belongings while the train crawled its way to Lahore, the capital of Punjab. The brick façade of Lahore station bristled with battlements, turrets and keeps as if the architect had designed it to withstand a siege.

They disembarked and gathered around Bill Skurr.

'I've booked rooms nearby,' he said. 'It'll be two days and a night before the Calcutta train pulls out.'

Clarence rubbed his hands. 'That'll give us a chance to explore the city.'

The hotel was only a five minute walk from the station. Even at this late hour, people crowded the roads. The crush of humans and animals added to Clarence's desire for a cool, empty room, and he anticipated having clean sheets and water.

Tucked into corners, well-wrapped bodies lay in low beds like camp cots.

'They're spilling out of their houses to escape the heat and catch some of the cool night air,' Bill said.

Clarence let his eyes wander over the mass of sleeping bodies. He bit his lip, thinking of the homeless he'd seen lying on the cold streets outside London's stations. 'I think they have nowhere else to sleep.'

Sanitary arrangements at the hotel were primitive. An enamel pot fitted into a wooden chair served as the toilet and flies buzzed around the half-filled chamber pots. The friends decided to use the facilities at the railway station instead as a sweeper regularly hosed the floors down.

A pear-shaped ceramic bowl sat level with the concrete floor with two large tiles in the shape of feet on both sides of the shallow receptacle and occupants had to squat with their boots planted on the giant feet.

At Lahore, breakfast exceeded their expectations as waiters served egg, bacon, toast, fresh butter, marmalade and fruit.

After their meal, they set out to explore the city. Stephen acted as guide. 'Lahore is a well laid-out town with both Mogul and colonial architecture,' he said. 'The bazaar, the fort, the station, the hotel and major buildings are all in Main Street.'

They followed the main road, which divided the old and new parts of Lahore. Tombs and mosques dotted the city. To the west, the bastions of Fort Lahore and the minarets of Emperor Aurangzeb's royal mosque dominated the skyline. The city's main thoroughfare led to the bazaars and, further on to the Kashmir Gate. Cow pats littered the unpaved streets and flies hovered overhead like a constant cloud. Fragrances of spices and incense from the temples and the overpowering odour of smoke from the cow dung fires hung in the air. The friends elbowed their way through the throng.

Streets throbbed with life. Along the roadside, barbers shaved their customers with an open blade. 'Wouldn't want to bump into a barber by mistake,' Clarence chuckled, holding a handkerchief to his nose to keep out the dust.

'No. He may slit his customer's throat,' Angus agreed.

They passed a man who held his head sideways while another peered into his ears.

'What's he doing?' Albert asked.

'Removing wax with a thin twisted wire that has a scoop at the end,' Stephen said.

A boy with deformed legs propelled himself along on a wooden-wheeled cart that squeaked and groaned on the dusty road. Beggars stared out of sightless eyes, arms stretched out, palms facing upwards.

Children besieged the friends. 'No poppa. No momma. No sister. No brother,' they chanted, patting their stomachs.

Clarence's heart ached for the children. He felt for his wallet.

'This is a common sight. Don't dig for your wallet every time you see a beggar or you'll be swamped by them,' Stephen warned.

Further on, they came to the administrative heart of the city. A brownish brick building, with towers and turrets, reminded Clarence of England. 'I wonder how the folk at home are faring.' He stopped and bought a newspaper from a wayside stall. Since leaving the ship, he'd been starved of news about the war.

'Not too good, I expect,' Stephen replied. 'My younger brothers and sisters were to evacuate to Canada, but Mother wrote saying that she couldn't bear the indefinite separation and sent them to the country instead.'

Clarence thought of his own brother Roy now safely ensconced in the countryside. 'Yes, one has a greater chance of surviving there.'

He shuddered, recalling the time he had seen an entire wall collapse over firemen who were trying to stem the blaze. The fire engine had exploded like a bomb. 'I can never forget the carnage. Houses completely wiped out; roads blocked by craters; telephones out of action; gas, water and electricity mains shattered.'

Stephen pulled them back to the present with a jolt. 'The heat here is not unlike the fires.'

'Let's visit Bikaner House,' Clarence said. 'It's where Rudyard Kipling used to live.' The author had written so much about India and brought the vast continent into life during his boyhood. 'Won't get this chance again, you know. These two big clock towers on the building can serve as a landmark.' He glanced back at the buildings stretching before him on Main Street.

'It would be a pity to miss such an opportunity, but we'll have to hire a gharry.' Stephen placed his forefingers into his mouth and gave a shrill whistle.

Two gharry *wallahs* whipped their bony ponies and raced each other. Their hooves clicked on the metalled road, raising sparks like fire crackers. They arrived together, the emaciated animals panting and sweating with the exertion.

Bill thrust his lip forward and scratched his head. 'I haven't the heart to turn one away. Let's split up and take both.'

Clarence smiled. Bill *did* have a soft spot after all.

They entered the carriage, which creaked with their weight. The interior was posh with cushioned seats and a mirror facing the front. The ponies broke into a trot and stopped in front of Bikaner House. It looked like the first storey of an unfinished mosque with its gothic arches springing from column to column around its façade.

Clarence took a photo with his Brownie box camera.

As the sun started to lose its intensity, they returned to the hotel. Paraffin lamps illuminated the wealthier merchants' shops. The poorer ones had a lighted wick that floated around in an earthenware dish shaped in the form of a kettle. Like Aladdin's lamp.

The following morning, Clarence tore a page off the calendar, revealing the date below—February 1. How time had flown! Only three months ago he had been in England. *How are my parents? Has Nottingham been bombed?* He sent up a brief prayer for them.

The whole of Lahore appeared to be at the station, trying to get aboard an already overloaded train. Locked doors did not deter those who had been waiting on the platform. They dived through windows of third-class carriages, balanced on the steps outside or hung on to the sides. Some clung to straps suspended from the ceiling. Others stood flattened against the wall or squatted on benches.

Fortunately, their carriage had *reserved* written on the door, and all means of entry remained locked until Bill produced their tickets.

The conductor hastened forward, unlocked the door and gave a reptilian bow. 'I will look after the *sahibs*.' He shook his head from side to side in rhythm with his voice and beat back his own countrymen with his staff to make way for them.

'Their caste system prompts this behaviour,' Stephen said.

Clarence nodded. 'We have a similar situation, only it's called *class*.'

The engine gave a warning toot and moved off. Clarence sat watching the country change from a dusty desert to a sandy plain, dotted with shrubs and trees. Perspiration streamed down his face despite the overhead fans.

Within a few hours, the brown countryside turned a dull green and the train came to a halt, its hissing and sputtering drowned by the racket of people trying to get on board. A loud bang at the door alerted them. Someone was attempting to enter their carriage.

The door opened but Angus stopped the intruder halfway by stretching out his booted foot and glaring at him.

A dark-skinned native in a British army uniform partly entered the reserved area. Angus forced him back.

'Let me sleep on the floor, *sahibs*. I can't get in anywhere. Please, *sahibs*. Please.' The soldier clasped his hands as he leaned forward into the compartment.

Everyone released a growl of disapproval and totally ignored him.

Eventually he turned away to search elsewhere. Clarence frowned, thinking of the Indian who was ready to shed his blood for England. *I ought to have stood up for the poor fellow and allowed him some floor space. One day we may have to staunch his wounds and carry him on a stretcher, but now, we didn't even provide him with a bit of room.*

That night, he dreamt of Gunga Din who he had seen in a movie of the same name. He woke up in a sweat. He should have done something for the chap.

Just before eight a.m., despite the crowded conditions, the train stopped for more passengers. Clarence woke to the sound of hammering on the door. Three airmen, their uniforms rank with perspiration, were trying to get in. The air force obviously hadn't provided a reserved compartment for the men even though the army had booked one for the FAU.

One glance brought back memories of the Blitz in England. The men were heroes.

'You're welcome,' Stephen said and they all nodded.

The tall airman indicated his two companions, 'Alan and Tim. I'm Shorty. We've been in hospital with malaria and are on our way back to our units.'

The men were sallow from the daily dose of mepacrine tablets. They remained on until the end of their journey, sleeping on the floor at nights.

After Lahore, the country grew greener, and when Clarence opened a window, no one protested.

All night the train rocked towards Calcutta. On both sides of the track, irrigation canals quenched sandy wastes and wells supported a chessboard of fields. Strings of camels plodded along, their haughty heads held high in the air, their backs laden with sugar cane.

The following day they passed through Lucknow, scene of the 1857 Indian Mutiny.

Clarence could not restrain himself. 'I'd love to visit the residency of Sir Henry Lawrence and see its battle-scarred walls, but we don't stop long enough for sight-seeing.'

Bill nodded. 'Have to leave that for some other time, chum.'

They crossed the Indus River at Allahabad and followed the Ganges Valley. Fields stretched for miles on the riverbanks. Corpses of diseased beggars and animal carcasses floated down the Ganges and the stench of death drifted into the carriage through the windows.

Despite the sickening odour, they gazed out of the window as the train clattered across the Dufferin Bridge. Steps lined the west bank and led down to the river at Benares.

Alan lit his cigarette. Inhaling deeply, he said, 'They are bathing *ghats* where bodies were cremated. When the wind blows in this direction you can smell the smoke. At dawn, pilgrims take their morning dip and the city becomes alive.'

A bloated cadaver of an animal floated along with the current. Vultures pecked at the eyes of a dilated human corpse.

Alan shrugged. 'Probably an untouchable with no relatives to give him a decent send off to the other world.'

Tim, who had so far remained silent, now chimed in. 'Benares is one of the most important places of pilgrimage in India.'

He paused and Shorty took up the threads of conversation. 'Thousands immerse themselves in the river and drink the water.'

Tim wiped his mouth with the back of his hand and continued. 'Relatives walk three times around a funeral pyre before setting it alight. Then they sprinkle the ashes into the Ganges. The river is covered with marigold petals and prayer leaves.'

'I'd rather visit the Taj Mahal,' Clarence replied, 'but I won't have time for sightseeing. I'm on my way to China.'

'Don't miss the Taj if you get the chance,' Tim said. 'One never knows what may happen.'

As the train approached their destination, hawkers got on to sell goods: children's toys, sweetmeats and cups of tea. A travelling entertainer played a sitar, while a child danced for the onlookers. It was difficult not to throw a coin or two. Clarence reached into his pocket, drew out a coin and threw it at her.

Stephen laughed. 'You'll soon learn not to do that too often.'

The following morning, the four men took turns to wash and shave in the small lavatory.

After a non-stop run on the western bank of the Hooghly River, they reached Calcutta's twin city, Howrah.

'My, my. Barrage-balloons,' Albert said.

Everyone's eyes turned heavenward. Two barrage balloons swam in the sky, glinting in the sun. Fear clutched at Clarence's heart. Somehow, they were so far away from England that the possibility of being bombed had seemed remote until that moment.

Around half past eleven, the train reached its terminus.

'This is where we get off.' Shorty swung his pack over his shoulder, then put out his hand. 'Thanks for letting us in.'

Alan and Tim followed and did the same.

William Duncumb and Harriet Vane, who ran the China Office in Calcutta, were at the station to meet the FAU. They exchanged pleasantries.

Harriet swatted a fly that kept buzzing around her face. 'These flies are most annoying, but you'll get used to them in time. We have them in China as well. I've just returned from there.' Although pale and washed-out, she worked efficiently, handing them a map indicating the position of their hotel and pointing out the best places for meals.

The station was a solid brick building with several towers each with a clock showing a different time. The ceiling was black with smoke from portable clay ovens that passengers used while waiting for the next train. Squatters huddled around pillars or lay on the wet floor, sound asleep.

'Howrah Station plays host to hordes of beggars,' William explained, as they pushed their way through beggers with outstretched arms, and coolies jostling for custom. 'Hang on to your bags. Don't let anyone get hold of them.'

He spent a few minutes bargaining with taxi drivers before beckoning to one. 'Some of you go with Harriet and the rest come with me.'

Clarence, Albert and Angus followed William.

Outside the station, the stream of humanity flowed past. Skinny rickshaw *wallahs* pulled people in hooded two-wheeled vehicles that looked like prams. Ponies, harnessed to wheeled boxes, laboured toward their destination. Men pushed bicycles loaded with merchandise of all kinds. Women balanced wares on their heads, and carried babies in their arms or toddlers on their hips.

'Now for a pleasant drive across the new cantilevered bridge into the city,' William said. 'We don't have far to go. The newly-opened Howrah Bridge connects Howrah and Calcutta. It's the world's busiest. In 1943, when India became a base for Allied military operations, it was unable to cope with the traffic.'

The chatter of the natives reached Clarence and a stray fly flew in through the window. Bullock carts lumbered along and bicycles wound their way among motorised vehicles. People clung to the open doors of double-decker buses. A heavy wind blew. Clarence glanced down at the muddy waters of the Hooghly. 'Is it true that the weight of passengers sometimes makes them keel over like yachts?'

'Yes, *sahib*. That's true,' the taxi driver agreed, rocking his head from side to side in Indian fashion.

No one except William had expected the betel-chewing individual to speak English and they glanced at each other in surprise.

Clarence hoped he would keep his eyes on the road and pay more attention to the traffic, but he got them to their destination despite playing chicken with the crowds.

After checking in at a hotel, they went out for lunch. The gutters overflowed with refuse accumulated since the last rains, and as they hurried along, the stench of urine and vomit followed, settling in their nostrils.

At the restaurant, the odour of spices was much more pleasant. A uniformed waiter ushered them to a table with two Americans who had been on board the *SS Strategist*. They had already managed to arrange for their flight across Burma into China, and were keen for action.

'It won't be long before we get to the little yellow bastards,' one said.

After lunch they parted and William Duncumb drove the India-bound party to the military tailors who measured them for tropical outfits.

Clarence joined the China group and spent most of the day at the Fort obtaining exit permits and the necessary papers. While waiting in the queue, he mentally went over Chinese words, repeating them to himself. Soon he would be off to the land of Marco Polo—devastated and torn since the Rape of Nanking.

He hoped to catch up with his friend Parry Davies over there.

His excitement rose to fever pitch.

CHAPTER 10

INDIA

Calcutta, February 1943

Within a few weeks after his arrival in India, Clarence sampled a curry that was fiery hot and brought tears to his eyes. Even drinking cold water did not ease the sensation. The whole day his stomach grumbled, fermenting like a vat of grapes in a wine vault. His interior bubbled and boiled, emitting foul gasses. He doubled up with abdominal cramps, passing blood in his stools. *What a fool I was to have tried those exotic dishes even though William had warned me to avoid them*, he thought.

His pale and worn looks prompted William Duncumb to take him to see Dr Napier at the Carmichael Hospital. 'This seems more like you've contracted dysentery, not simple diarrhoea,' he said, as he drove to the hospital.

The staff placed Clarence in a ward with eight other patients. Except for lights out at half past nine, there were no restrictions apart from his diet. But after having lived through three years of rationing in England, Clarence didn't complain.

In the morning, a tiny Indian nurse tripped in, pushing a trolley loaded with trays of eggs and toast for breakfast. 'That's all you'll get this morning,' she said. 'No bacon or sausages.'

At lunchtime she brought in a dish of fish, potatoes and vegetables, and in the evening, she placed a bowl of chicken stew on his bedside table. The nurse also handed out a couple of oranges and some milk between meals.

'You're feeding us like kings,' Clarence said. 'We don't get this in wartime England.'

The nurse adjusted her cap and smiled. 'You must keep up your strength. I'll bring you a bowl of custard and buttered toast for supper.'

After five days in hospital and a series of blood tests and x-rays, the doctors released Clarence, who immediately sent a cable to FAU Headquarters in China, requesting instructions. They advised him to postpone his departure, until his bouts of diarrhoea stopped.

Albert and Angus beamed at the news. Their six-week training at Manor Farm and the London Blitz had bonded the three friends. Clarence shared a room with them at Wood Street. William Duncumb and Chris Barber also resided in the same street.

The day after Clarence received the reply from China, William accompanied the three friends to the markets. Sacred cattle, garlanded by marigolds, butted their way through the throng, grazing on bananas laid out for sale. Flies, droning the threat of dysentery, descended on the food. Hawkers waved them off, sending them swarming to the next vendor. Shops displayed bolts of vibrant silks, colourful cotton, ready-made garments, jewellery, cane furniture and glassware. Sellers shouted out, extolling their wares. Buyers haggled over prices.

The four friends roamed in the bazaar, overpowered by the smell of dung and the aromatic odours of spices.

'Despite its filth and squalor, Calcutta, the home of India's poets and artists is a city with a soul,' William said.

Clarence reached forward to pick up a painted vase when a bell sounded above the noise and clamour. The booming of a gong followed. He froze. *Was it an air raid warning signal?*

William shook his head. 'Nothing to be alarmed about. It's simply a temple bell calling people for prayer. You'll get used to all this sooner or later.'

Clarence helped pack supplies for stations in China at Wood Street, while the sounds of traffic and the noise of hawkers carried through the open window. During his sojourn in Calcutta, prominent Indians like Mrs Nehru, wife of Congress member Pandit Nehru, sometimes dropped in at the office. Clarence regarded all men as God's children, so he felt at ease talking to dignitaries. It made no difference to him whether he spoke to the lowest caste labourer or someone in high office.

Life in India, away from the frontline and danger, was comparatively comfortable. At times, Chris and Clarence drove in the FAU's old Morris to the Victoria docks. The car plunged into a pandemonium of pedestrians, animals and vehicles, passing natives chewing lime wrapped in betel leaves and squirting scarlet juice on the pavements. The betel leaves acted as a narcotic, and natives chewed them as a relaxant for much the same reason they smoked their native cheerots.

At the docks, the scream of winches and the rattle of cranes deafened Clarence and the sweltering heat smothered him.

Chris mopped his brow. 'This is nothing. Within the next couple of months Calcutta becomes a hell-hole.'

Clarence also accompanied Chris when he drove the battered vehicle to meet volunteers at the railway station. Calcutta teemed with beggars who swamped them at the station.

'Both Moslems and Hindus believe in giving alms to obtain divine favour,' Chris explained. He had been in India for a few months and knew the customs of the two major religions.

Clarence nodded. 'Yes, William told me that begging has become a profession and that some parents deliberately blind or maim their child to elicit compassion.'

'I know your heart bleeds to witness such hardship but giving alms to a beggar encourages them to pester you more than ever,' Chris said.

A few days after this, when Clarence gave one *pice*, the smallest Indian currency, to a little child, hordes of children besieged him and tugged at his clothes, pleading for more. A small urchin stood on tiptoe and groped in

Clarence's shirt pocket, searching for coins.

Clarence, amazed at such rude behaviour, brushed him off. From then on, he refrained from dropping a few coppers into their suppliant hands, despite his longing to alleviate their sufferings.

Once Clarence and his two friends had settled in, William drove them to the area around Calcutta Fort. 'In 1756, Indians attacked the fort and imprisoned survivors in an underground cellar,' he said. 'All but a handful of the prisoners died of heat and suffocation overnight.'

'The Black Hole?' Clarence asked.

'Yes. When Britain built a much stronger fort later on, workers cleared the surrounding jungle. The clearing is known as the *Maidan*.' William waved his arm towards the long grassy park flanked by the avenue of trees. 'It's now used as a camp for our soldiers stationed in Calcutta.'

A sea of tents stretched over the area. Men in uniform lounged around, drinking cups of tea. A temporary airstrip had been set up on the *Maidan*. The aircraft bays were on a branch road that led to the shopping centre on Chowringhee Road, about two hundred yards away.

The Victoria Memorial, a massive marble-domed building, dominated the skyline. The imposing statue of Queen Victoria—a solid reminder of British Calcutta—stood regally at the entrance. The scent of marigolds wafted across the lawns as they paused and admired the edifice before entering.

'It looks very much like the Taj Mahal from pictures I've seen of it,' Clarence said.

William nodded. 'The building is made of the same type of marble as the Taj. It's built in a similar style, although not quite as magnificent.'

He guided them northwards, along Chowringhee Road. 'This is the city's oldest shopping avenue. To the right is the Grand Hotel, Calcutta's equivalent of Raffles in Singapore. Further on is Mission Row.'

At the corner of Dalhousie Square, he paused and glanced up at St Andrew's Church. 'It's locked. Sorry we can't go in.'

They stood for a while before the church, and William pointed to the General Post Office that partially covered the remains of the old fort. 'In the northeast corner of the building, a black marble tablet is used to mark the actual site of the Black Hole.'

'Where's the slab now?' Clarence asked.

'In July 1940, Chandra Bose lobbied for its removal, so the government moved it to the graveyard of St. John's Church.'

Fragments of original arches lining the east wall of the fortification still stood, a grim reminder of the Indian Mutiny. Clarence sank down on a tree stump. In his mind he heard the wail of despair that arose from more than a hundred long-dead throats. William, Angus and Albert left him to ponder on the past and strolled towards the river to get a better view of the famous Howrah Bridge.

After a short space of time, Clarence re-joined them and they returned to their lodgings, each wrapped in his own thoughts.

To his dismay, Clarence discovered that the chairs were alive with bugs that lived in every crevice and cranny. Flat, black and oval-shaped, they swelled up after sucking his blood. Their bites brought on an intense itching.

At cinemas and at church, he was not free of the vermin. Whenever one crawled on his thigh, his hands would roam over the seat until he found the bug and squashed it between his thumb and forefinger. If he was not careful, blood would spurt out, staining his fingers and leaving a red mark on his clothes.

One evening at the cinema, Angus fidgeted in his chair. Clarence opened his mouth to say something, but he thought better of it and remained silent. Soon after, he too was squirming. Something settled on his bare arms. He slapped his arm, thinking it was a mosquito. The slap resounded like a clap of thunder.

People turned around to glare at him.

Angus leaned forward. 'What was that?' Within two seconds, he, too, found a bloated bug on his arm. He snatched at it with his thumb and forefinger.

'Don't squash it,' Albert said—too late.

Blood spurted on Albert's face. His voice rose. 'I told you not to do that. William warned us not to crush them with our fingers.' He took out his handkerchief and dabbed his eye.

Someone rattled the seat behind him. 'If you guys can't pipe down, get your arses out of here.'

Not wishing to be involved in a fight, they settled down to watch the rest of the film.

Later, while examining his clothes, Clarence's eyes alighted upon the evening procession of cockroaches. He trampled on them until they scattered off in all directions. Each night they returned in force to renew the fray. It was a losing battle.

Once a week the *dhobi*—or washerman—carted away bags of dirty linen and washed them at a nearby stream, beating the clothes clean on a flat rock. He returned them neatly ironed and pure white the following week.

Jadu wallahs—or sweepers—were indispensable, but Hindus considered them untouchables, only permitting them to live a distance from the main village. *Jadu wallahs* laboured in the lowest jobs, cleaned toilets and swept garden paths and pavements. Industrious workers, they kept the place clean and put both hands to their heads in *salaam* whenever an Englishman passed.

Clarence never failed to acknowledge their greeting with a nod.

Dysentery and other tropical diseases like malaria and typhus were major problems—snakebites and dog bites, common occurrences. Rabies was rife in India. Dogs staggered on the streets, foaming at the mouth.

Once when Clarence and William were visiting a friend in hospital, they noticed a tightly-secured ward. 'That's the rabies ward,' William said. 'It's always kept locked. Unless an anti-rabies serum is administered in the early stages, the sickness is fatal. Patients have spasms and refuse to drink. They bark and try to bite people. Be wary of any suspicious-looking canine.'

Clarence vowed never to venture near a dog in India.

At Easter, William spent the weekend at Ramgarh with the Seagrave Unit, having worked with Dr Seagrave in 1941 during the fighting in Burma.

On his return, he told Clarence that he was leaving the FAU.

'How can you leave the Friends when they've done so much to help us conscientious objectors?' Clarence asked. 'A contract is binding, both legally and morally, and it's wrong to break your word.'

'I'm not breaking my word and enlisting in the army,' William replied. 'I'm re-joining Seagrave who's always in the frontline, tending to the wounded. The FAU is willing to release me from my contract.'

Clarence had regarded William as his mentor in India, and was disappointed he was leaving before his time had expired. But Allied troops were getting ready to advance into Burma, and Clarence realised that William didn't want to be left behind. He, too, strained at the bit like a warhorse, wanting to join the fray in China, but his weak stomach still held him back in India.

As the year passed from Easter to Christmas, Clarence came to learn something of the two major religions in India. At first he had been dismayed at the sight of countless cesspools, drains teeming with rats, cow dung and human faeces on the roads. In time, however, he saw beyond the wretchedness and lost himself in a world of mystery where snake charmers kissed cobras, fire-eaters swallowed flames and *sadus* walked on live coals.

During the festival of Holi, Hindus danced and sang in a spirit of abandon. They threw coloured powder or water on each other, turning hair and clothes a mottled red.

At Ramadan, Muslims kept a strict fast, neither eating nor drinking from sunrise to sunset.

Clarence marvelled at the differences between Hindus and Muslims.

The former believed in several deities and the latter, in one God with Mohammed as their prophet. No wonder they often fought among themselves.

When the golden hues of autumn began to turn into a fairyland of falling leaves in shades of red, orange and yellow, Clarence's thoughts flew home. It pained him to think of how well he ate, while his family lived on meagre rations. A sense of guilt overcame him, but in his heart, he knew his mother would never begrudge him the luxuries he indulged in. He posted home some tins of butter and a dozen eggs preserved in lime. Clarence did this whenever he could.

Winter ushered in Dewali, the Hindu Festival of Lights. As the three friends were curious to know about Hinduism, Chris Barber took them to visit a temple dedicated to the goddess Kali. It reeked with the stench of blood from animal sacrifices. Pilgrims queued before a half-naked *sadu*, who held a bowl containing saffron-coloured powder and imprinted their foreheads with it.

Chris moved on to pause before the black-faced deity. It held a severed human head dripping with gore, while it stuck out a bloated tongue from its ravenous mouth.

Clarence swallowed hard. 'Their god looks more like a devil.'

A stench of blood pervaded the temple. Clarence recalled William's words, 'At times it's not uncommon for humans to be sacrificed to Kali, even though the practise has been banned.' He shuddered and turned green. 'This place gives me the creeps. Let's get out of here.'

That evening, Clarence, who generally possessed a good appetite, only had a bowl of soup for dinner.

Hindus celebrated during the five-day festival, devouring *rosgullas*, a speciality of the city. Mixed with milk, wheat and lentils, the dessert was fried before being drenched in sweet syrup. Clarence indulged his palate and developed a liking for them. He loved the cloying sweetness of the reddish-brown balls that slid down his throat. As he bit into them, he was reminded of the high teas he had enjoyed on a visit to Scotland.

At nights, buildings were illuminated by colourful lanterns, firecrackers spluttered and rockets streaked across the black sky. They continued to live as if the war didn't even exist.

Would England ever return to normal?

Only snippets of information from home crept through on the wireless or the grapevine—some true, but all unreliable. Letters were lost to the deep. Reports of enemy planes attacking the midlands were sufficient to bring a frown to Clarence's already stern face as he listened to the radio. His thoughts spun, nearly careering out of orbit with concern for his family in Nottingham.

How were they faring? He visualised them running for shelter at every mournful wail of the sirens: his mother grabbing a book, a box of matches, a kettle of hot water and an overcoat to ward off the cold. Her arthritis troubled her especially on wet winter days. Clarence imagined her rubbing her knees with linament.

She was the mainstay of the family and would pull them through any ordeal, but he could not help thinking the worst. He had seen it all in London. The dead and dying— the damage stray bits of blazing shrapnel were capable of inflicting.

***

Back in London, Ada's thoughts were with her son and she sat down to write a four-page epistle to Clarence. She enclosed a pound note as a Christmas present, knowing the FAU received no wages,

The next morning, she set out early to post the letter and then joined the queue at the local butcher with their meat rations. With Roy at boarding school, Doug in the army and Clarence abroad, she still had four mouths to feed – her husband, Stan, Eva and herself. As a guard in the railways, Watson was busy day and night, transporting troops from one destination to another. Stan worked in a plane factory during the day and was on ARP duties at nights. Eva had commenced nurses' training, and asserted her independence although she still lived at home. Her daughter had always been a rebel, and no amount of spanking could tame her.

Her mind drifted to her two sons – Clarence, who was on his way to India and Doug, who now fought in North Africa. *Dear Lord,* she prayed, *do protect my children. I've lived through one war and know how it affects lives. Take my life if you like, but please don't cut short their young ones.*

The butcher interrupted her thoughts. 'What can I do for you, ma'm?'

Hastily, Ada put in her order, collected her meagre rations and returned home. Later on, she had a prayer meeting to attend and a sewing circle for older women, where she knitted socks for boys in the frontline. Not for *her* sons. She'd already provided them with all the winter gear they needed, but for others. She recalled the days when Watson had been fighting in the trenches of Europe and shuddered. 'Thank God he's safe at home now,' she muttered.

The sewing circle carried on later than usual and darkness had already crept in when Ada wended her way home. She wrapped her scarf tighter around her neck and paused before Mrs Black's door. *Should I drop in to console her for the recent loss of her son?*

She knocked, and a weeping Mrs Black invited her inside. Ada put her arms around her friend's shoulder and held her close until the sobs subsided. 'Shall I make you a cup of tea?' she asked, and without waiting for a reply, she put a kettle on the stove.

Total darkness prevailed by the time Ada left her friend's house. She hastened her steps. The German raiders would arrive before she got home if she didn't hurry.

The moon rose, and gratefully, she picked her way homewards.

She was right. Within a few minutes sirens screamed. Ada ran towards the nearest public air raid shelter. A pain stabbed her chest. She tripped and fell, dropping her sewing basket and scattering its contents.

The figure of a boy darted from the shadows and snatched a pair of socks. Half rising to her feet, Ada stretched out her hand and grabbed the boy. 'Oh no you don't!'

'I only wanted to keep my feet warm,' the lad replied. 'I'm going to watch the dog fights, and it's cold out here.'

Still clinging to the thief's arm, Ada rose to her feet. She held him with a vice-like grip. At fifty-three, she was still strong and her voice powerful. 'Help me pick up my things and come with me to the air raid shelter.'

Subdued, the boy helped Ada and followed her into the already-crowded shelter. She made her way to the water tank and drank a mug of water, remaining quiet until the pain subsided and her breathing settled down. 'Why aren't you at home, lad?'

'I have no home, m'am. Our house was bombed during the Blitz last May.'

'Where do you live now then?'

'I stay with a few other kids in a deserted house. At nights, we watch the dogfights and in the mornings we collect the shrapnel that falls from overhead.'

'Don't you know it's dangerous?'

'My mother and grandma didn't go out at nights, but they died from the raids all the same.'

Ada's heart swelled with pity. 'Come and stay with me. My two sons are overseas and you can make a home with us until they return. We have an Anderson shelter. You'll be safe with us.' She sounded confident but she knew it wouldn't survive a direct hit.

The young waif shook his head. 'We're free where we are. We don't have to go to school, and we're all orphans, so no one misses us.'

When the all-clear sounded the boy slipped away before Ada could restrain him. She was aware that many such children lived in bombed-out residences. Whole tenements had been wiped out during the Nottingham Blitz in May 1941. *The bombers are not likely to target homes that have already been destroyed. Perhaps they were safer where they were. Who knows! The Lord had promised to take care of the sparrow that fell from its nest. These children were more precious than sparrows to Him.*

Fires from burning buildings lit her way back as she returned home. She unlocked the front door and fell into a chair, exhausted. *Thank you Lord for sparing my home,* she breathed.

***

Ada's letter did not reach Clarence until February when an aerograph arrived at the FAU office in Wood Street. To lighten the load of letters for soldiers at the front, the Post Office had photocopied and reduced them in size before despatching by plane.

Clarence turned the mail over and recognised his mother's writing. A glow of warmth seeped through his body as he read her letter. A smile replaced his frown.

Clarence clutched the mail to his heart. *At least they had got through safely!*

Within a few weeks the heat in Calcutta was stifling and the dry and dusty wind stirred. Once the sun had set, Clarence took a walk in the *Maidan,* hoping to cool down. He hurried back to the hostel, hoping the postman had brought in some mail from home. Waiting for him was a longed-for letter from Doug. He climbed the stairs, two at a time, intending to savour the news alone in his room. He removed his drenched clothing, took a shower and turned on the fans. His fresh shirt soon grew damp with the perspiration that ran down his face and dripped into his eyes. Clarence sank into a chair, wiped his eyes and slit open the crumpled envelope, assuring himself that his brother must be well if he was able to write.

CHAPTER 11

DOUG

North Africa, November 1940

The war had not yet taken a serious turn in Africa, and the Italians were their only opponents when Doug arrived in Egypt. His initial excitement of seeing new places gave way to boredom. Only a ridge separated British troops from the enemy, and Doug's only entertainment was to sit outside his tent and watch the sunset while sipping tea.

Each day a solitary RAF plane flew over to reconnoitre the area. Once, when the plane failed to return, an Italian pilot flew over, buzzed the camp and circled over the crashed site until a British rescue party left to rescue the wounded airmen.

It wasn't long before Doug's division was posted out to the frontline. They were soon forced to retreat to Salem, a town just within Egypt. During the fighting, Doug was struck by shrapnel from a German shell. The force of nearby explosions crushed his helmet. He lost consciousness.

When he regained his senses, the smell of cordite, scorched flesh and smoke choked him. Pursing his lips, he tried to spit a foul taste from his mouth but his tongue was too dry. Sand and dust covered his face and nose. Helpless in the blazing sun, he blinked to clear his vision but there was so much grit under his lids.

A nearby tank burst into flames, sending showers of dirt and shrapnel in all directions. Had he been hit again? He puked from the stench of gore. Flies swarmed in clouds, feasting on his blood and vomit. All attempts to shake them off failed.

Dizzy from the force of explosions, he slipped back into unconsciousness.

When Doug's brain cleared, a red dusk mantled the desert. It had turned bitterly cold and his teeth chattered. He had cast off his greatcoat in the heat of battle and the noonday sun, but now he bit his lips and longed for it.

Both sides lit flares. His eyes focussed on a couple of soldiers sprawled a few yards away from the smouldering ruins of guns and vehicles. Crawling towards them, he stretched out his hands and touched their warm and sticky bodies.

They did not respond to his shaking.

Worn out from loss of blood and unable to get to his feet, he collapsed among the dead and dying men, waiting for help. For the first time since he had enlisted, he grew fearful. The excitement of war had drugged his imagination, making him incapable of seeing danger, pain or death. He tried to gather up the strands of his thoughts, to think of words to instil courage. *Gallantry, decency, honour, England.*

He remained in a white trance of fear, unable to utter a sound or move his aching body. Machine guns hammered behind him. Grenades flashed and exploded in all directions. Two Italians rushed past with fixed bayonets, their plumed helmets waving in the breeze. Sherwood Foresters ran around him. He recognised them by their green socks and tried to call out for help but no sound issued from his dry lips. He waved his arms. Too late. All his attempts to rise failed. Exhausted, he fell back on the sand. A shell whistled by, exploding a few yards away.

A bespectacled young man appeared above Doug and felt his pulse. His protective big brother Clarence was here to care for him, as he'd always done.

Clarence reached out and pressed his brother's hand. 'I'm here, Doug. It's me. I've got you. I'll look after you. Hold on.'

Darkness invaded Doug's mind once more.

A sudden stop jolted Doug back to consciousness. He looked around and found himself on a stretcher. Two men laid it carefully on the ground.

Covered by bloodstained blankets and flies, a line of wounded stretched for several yards on the bare desert. Some lay on their sides, vomiting, their uniforms soiled by urine and faeces. *How different everyone looks*, Doug thought. Before the battle, he'd changed into clean shirts, socks and underwear because of the possibility of infection. He'd shaved carefully in case of facial wounds. Despite all these morbid precautions, he was still unprepared for what followed.

A convoy of trucks drew up, carrying more casualties and orderlies laid them down on the sand to await their turn for treatment.

Doug fell into a stupor and awoke in a field hospital. Wind whipped the canvas walls of the large tent. Slowly, he moved his head and licked his lips. Weak and thirsty from loss of blood, unable to move his body, his eyes swept the surroundings.

Two rows of beds ran along the sides. The sun poured in, filling the tent like a glass of champagne. A nurse, humming softly, bent over her patients. The floor was covered by mats but the wind had blown the sand in, making it gritty.

The crunch of boots alerted Doug that someone was approaching.

'You've lost a lot of blood and were beginning to hallucinate,' the medic murmured. 'You need rest but you'll be fine in a few weeks.'

Doug shut his eyes, glad he was in friendly hands. For days his mind escaped from the harness of sanity and ran wild in delirium, reliving the slow slide of the time when they had waited for the fighting to commence—the grumbling, cursing and the constant drilling. He groaned aloud.

A form loomed over him. 'Feeling sick? In pain? Need a shot of morphine?'

'No. I'm all right.'

'What's wrong then?' The figure moved closer. 'Cough it up and get it out of your system. You'll feel better for it.'

'Where's my brother, Clarence? He was with me last night— or last week.'

The attendant placed his hand on Doug's shoulder. 'Sorry, old chap.

You've been hallucinating. You're going to be transferred from the field hospital to a military infirmary away from the fighting. Doctors will remove the shrapnel.'

He plunged a needle into Doug's arm.

For weeks, Doug could only limp around in the infirmary feeling sorry for himself. His main problem had been loss of blood, leaving him dehydrated and exhausted.

As soon as he was able to walk without support, he received orders to be ready to board the first batch of trucks for rest and recuperation in Cairo. He collected a new set of clothes from the quartermaster, had a haircut and a bath.

After receiving his pay and leave pass, Doug limped over to the waiting vehicles and looked for his truck. Drawing out the retaining pins, he let the rear door drop with a clatter and stepped back as dust arose in small clouds from the mudguard.

He clambered aboard the three-tonner with some assistance from the driver and slumped down on a wooden slatted seat with thirteen others. Some of the men had handkerchiefs wrapped around their faces. The non-commissioned officer sat in front next to the driver, who had helped everyone aboard, then secured the tailgate.

Once they left camp, the truck picked up speed. The men swayed as they swept around bends in the road, sand spewing from the truck's spinning wheels. The sun beat down, but fortunately, a dark green canvas cover served as a roof. Whenever the vehicle hit a pothole, the occupants bounced in their seats and dust billowed in.

Doug grimaced. 'This is sheer hell,' he groaned.

'Hang on to the sides and lean on me,' the soldier next to him said. 'It may ease your pain.'

'Thanks. I'll do that if you don't mind.' Doug leant against him and sighed.

The jarring ride continued until finally, the truck slowed down and stopped at their destination.

'You can hop out now, but wait for the driver to help you down.'

'Thanks, chum.'

They booked in for seven nights at the Kitchener House Pension. Doug looked forward to a good night's rest, but the cotton blanket was insufficient to keep out the cold, and lodgers kept coming in at all hours during the night. Many were drunk and rowdy, dropping their boots with a loud thud on the bare wooden floor, and paying scant consideration to those already in bed.

Doug groaned and turned over. Well past midnight, he fell asleep.

He awoke late the next day and caught a gharry to the Tipperary Club, the hub of entertainment. Soon a feud arose. Rival regiments and divisions threw bottles and smashed furniture. Doug kept clear of the fray and left before the redcaps arrived. All he wanted was to get well.

When his energy returned, he spent his time visiting the markets and buying silk stockings, scarves, neckties and handkerchiefs for his family. He even took an organised tour to Memphis. There, the colossal statue of Ramses II gazed down as it had done for centuries.

On his last day, Doug went to the rendezvous where trucks were waiting to take the whole leave party back to camp. Before leaving, he handed a letter for Clarence to an ambulance worker, who was returning to Calcutta for rest and recuperation. He refrained from mentioning his injury in case Clarence worried unduly for him, but he told him of the capture of his general and staff officers during the retreat.

Doug was posted to Tobruk on light duties. An Australian division was also stationed at Tobruk harbour, and Doug enjoyed how clipped English voices mingled with thick Australian accents. He was surprised to hear the Australians call everyone a bastard. Their friendly tones, however, rarely gave any offence. Besides, they feared nothing and fought bravely. One of them taught him how to swim. His name was Jim.

'Come on, mate. Don't just stand in the water. Just relax,' he said.

Within a few days, Doug, too, was swimming—not like a fish—but at least he could stay afloat and move forward.

'Now we'll swim to your destroyer and use its wreck as a diving board.'

Doug enjoyed himself in the water, watching dogfights whenever a German aircraft flew over, attempting to photograph their position.

When British troop carriers brought in fresh troops and supplies to relieve the siege of Tobruk, Doug and his division returned with the wounded to the Abbassia barracks in the suburbs of Cairo.

On 24 June, newspapers announced the fall of Tobruk. The Allies had withstood the siege for so long, but combined Italian and German forces proved too great for them. Doug was shocked.

The following month, he was assigned to drive General John Harding in his armoured car.

Elated at his promotion, Doug no longer felt like a raw recruit. He bore his hardships with grace, even when flies targeted his eyes, nose or mouth, and gathered every drop of moisture from his perspiration.

Driving across the desert, the convoy frequently passed herds of mangy-looking camels grazing on the thorny scrub. They uttered moos like cows with sore throats.

When the shelling stopped the silence was profound. Doug loved watching the first hint of dawn come blushing up the horizon. As the sun rose, it revealed palms, olives and fig trees surrounding sky-blue pools and bright yellow blooms of broom bushes. At times they passed camel caravans with their riders wrapped up to the eyes as a protection from the sand. The general then ordered a halt, and the cook went about exchanging tea and sugar for camel's milk and eggs with the natives. Cook then cleaned the mudguard and grilled the eggs on it. The sun was so hot he didn't even need a fire!

The heat was unbearable with the sun burning on the bare steel. If the windscreen was left open to get some air in, the sand blew into the men's faces. Dust travelled in a cloud and spirals of sand a few feet high danced dizzily before them almost blacking out the sun.

They passed graves marked by crosses jammed into sand-filled petrol tins, as well as burned out trucks and tanks. Once they stopped at an abandoned enemy tank, and Doug found a case containing a pair of field glasses, but the leather disintegrated at his touch.

By the end of October 1942, Montgomery launched the Second Battle of El Alamein at midnight. When the Eighth Army broke through enemy lines, dusty and bloody Italian soldiers with field dressings on their faces waved white towels in surrender. Some clutched canteens of water as they trudged towards Allied troops.

After the battle, Doug wandered over to the Italian prisoner of war camp. Finding them cooking their evening meal of soup, pasta and beans, he offered them cigarettes and tins of bully beef in exchange for Italian souvenirs. When a penknife with a relief of a steel-helmeted Mussolini caught his attention, he pointed to it. The Italian wiped his hands on his trousers and handed over the knife.

On 23 January 1943, after travelling nearly one thousand and four hundred miles, the Eighth Army captured Tripoli. The wireless blared out that Rommel had returned to Germany with jaundice after the fall of the city, and a few days later, Axis generals began surrendering.

In May 1943, after three years of desert warfare, German and Italian troops laid down their arms. Planes and ambulances evacuated the seriously wounded and all ranks were authorised seven days' leave before the infantry began its trek back to Cairo.

On his arrival at Cairo Doug did guard duties at a Transit Camp while recovering from an attack of desert sores on his back. He had suffered irritants like toe rot and sweat rash but this was far worse. Before leaving with the Seventh Armoured Division for Salerno in Italy, Doug posted his letter to Clarence, who was still in India, awaiting his transfer to China. He enclosed a copy of the *Eighth Army News* and the *Crusader*.

***

Back in India, Clarence flicked through the pages of a newspaper, only reading the headlines. *The battle for North Africa is over, but when will the war in Europe end?* Dysentery no longer sent Clarence scurrying to the toilet, and the sight of food now enhanced, rather than diminished, his appetite. His strength had returned, making him physically strong enough to face whatever awaited him across the mountains in the Far East. As the weeks passed, blighted hopes began to stir and he grew restless. *Dear God,* he prayed, *please send me soon to that vast mass of suffering humanity.*

CHAPTER 12

DEATH IN THE FAMILY

Calcutta, March 1943

As the year progressed, Clarence experienced the seasonal cycles within the vast continent. In March, a bank of dark clouds appeared. Winds tore up and tossed trees to the ground, stripping and carrying off top soil. Dust seeped through closed shutters. Skins shrivelled and eyelids grew paper-thin. The earth became a breathless furnace. Even late in the evenings, the heat was stifling. As fans whirred above, Clarence tossed in bed at nights, throwing off his sheets. He consumed copious amounts of water with a teaspoon of salt—surprisingly refreshing on a hot day, helping replace the minerals lost through sweat.

During the FAU's first medical check in India, the doctor had warned all members, 'Whatever you do, don't get the clap.'

But their needs outstripped caution. Latent carnal cravings grew uncontrollable as men visited the marketplace where pimps accosted likely customers.

'You want boy? You want girl?' the pimps asked. 'Very beautiful. Very clean.'

Clarence gritted his teeth and waved them off, just as he brushed off flies, resisting the temptation to give in to his sensual desires. He couldn't betray Mary.

At the end of the month, the sky turned to a pewter grey and trees appeared dark and solemn. A flash of lightning zigzagged across followed by a clap of thunder and the first few raindrops sank into the dust, devoured by the thirsty earth.

'Indra, the god of thunder, has loosened his arrows,' Indians said, dancing with joy.

The weather remained hot between bursts of rain, and the humidity became even more unbearable than the dry heat. The damp heat set up a sweat that saturated their uniforms. Clothes hanging in cupboards accumulated patches of green. A dank odour arose in houses and shoes gathered mould overnight.

The thermometer crept up and prickly heat covered everyone like a hair shirt. Clarence tried hard not to scratch the blisters on his body, and in-between showers, he sprinkled himself with talcum powder to relieve the itching.

To top it all, Doug hadn't written for a long time. Clarence's worries increased.

It wasn't until July that Clarence received a steady stream of letters from Doug saying that everyone awaited *the big show*. On two occasions apparently Doug's lorry had burst into flames and he had escaped from burns, but now he suffered from desert sores on his neck.

Clarence shuddered at the thought of his brother caught in the fire. He visualised him enveloped by flames, screaming and hurling himself from the vehicle.

He rose and shook his head. He must put away such thoughts. He knew the big show meant the Allied advance in North Africa. He sympathised with Doug and, involuntarily, he scratched the prickly heat on his own neck. He continued reading.

A feather of anxiety rose as he read the words: *I haven't heard from Mam for a few weeks.*

No mail had come in from her either. Had his mother's letters been torpedoed at sea? Was all well at home?

Three days later, an envelope with a black border arrived. *Was Doug dead? Perhaps Stan had died during an air raid.* Clarence trembled as he tore open the envelope and unfolded the note. It was from Michael Cadbury of Manor Farm informing him of his mother's death. She had passed away on Monday 25 May after being ill for only a few hours.

Clarence dropped the letter on his lap and shut his eyes. It must have been her heart. She worked too hard and worried so much. With a racing pulse, he picked up the note and continued reading. A friend had brought his mother home when she collapsed after giving a talk at a church meeting. She had died soon after. Thirty-six wreaths had surrounded the coffin.

Clarence's heart twisted in agony. Tears obscured his vision, knowing he would never see his mother again. *Was this why my heart has weighed so heavily recently?* A sob escaped him. His beloved mother was only fifty-four, but worries for her family had caused her heart to break. Two wars had been too much for her to bear. With bent head, he bowed to the Almighty. Now the Nazis were powerless to harm his mother.

***

Meanwhile, back in Nottingham, Eva, who still lived with her parents after her marriage, took over running the household. Unlike her brothers, she'd never gotten on well with her mother, whom she'd considered too strict. Eva had disliked her mother's Bible-bashing and she wanted her own way in all things.

Now that Ada had passed away, she realised how much Ada had been doing for the family – cooking, cleaning and making the house a home. Her heart ached to witness her grieving father whose hair turned white overnight. The house remained in breathless silence. No more did she hear his cheery voice break into song, or have to put up with her mother's scolding, asking her to help in the kitchen.

If only she'd spent more time with her mother, she'd be a better cook now. All she could do were stews with their meat rations. How did she manage to stretch their food rations to satisfy their appetites? In a way, it was fortunate her father was too worn with grief to notice the absence of his wife's magical touch at mealtimes.

Eva continued her nursing duties, doing her bit for Britain. In her spare time she scrounged the kitchen shelves for cooking books and tried new recipes to tempt her father's appetite.

At times her thoughts turned to Clarence. She knew he'd feel this loss deeply. On her first free day from work, she sat down and wrote a letter to Clarence full of sympathy for not being able to make it for their mother's funeral.

Eva had been fortunate as her husband, Albert, had obtained leave from action in France to attend the funeral. She had deliberately sent a telegram to him saying, 'Mum died', hoping his superior officers would think it was *his* mother who'd died.

Albert didn't enlighten them of their error, and he was able to get away from the frontline and spend a few precious days with her.

* * *

Mary Flintoff had read about Ada Dover's death in the papers. She attended the burial service and wept; not so much for Ada, but for Clarence. How painful it must have been for him to be unable to attend his mother's funeral.

Her heart missed a beat as she thought of their walk home that night, long ago—his strong arms about her; the soft kisses that had grown more intense as they drew nearer her home. She had hoped he'd ask her to marry him, but he'd departed without a word of marriage. Would he, too, dream of the last dance they'd had before he left for China?

When Mary heard that his ship had stopped in India she was consumed with worry. What if he met some Indian beauty who used her wiles to seduce him? Or he fell in love with another girl? Her friend Ethel Snow had boasted about corresponding with him.

Why had she quarrelled with Clarence over registering himself as a conscientious objector? The two of them had so much in common and she had let him slip through her hands! Their only difference in opinion had been their attitudes toward war.

Mary had now risen to the rank of lieutenant in the Girls' Training Corps. She loved the smart blue and white uniform and the peak cap, tilted to the right. Her heart had beaten fast as she learned how to tap out messages in Morse code, study first aid and map reading. She stood tall when they sang *Jerusalem* and *Land of Hope and Glory*, and her eyes moistened.

Did Clarence, too, thrill at the rousing songs in praise of England as she did? She knew he did. Conscientious objectors were seen as unpatriotic and cowardly, but she realised that Clarence loved his country. She consoled herself that even though he was a pacifist, he wasn't an Absolutist. She couldn't bear them. They refused to co-operate with the government by declining to take any form of alternative service. They even refused to wear khaki and help in the Medical Corps as it would only relieve another man to serve in the army and kill others!

She must not let him forget her. Little darts of happiness shot through her body as she thought of him. The Lord had made them for each other and she had to write to him before it was too late.

Mary contacted the Friends Ambulance Unit at Birmingham and asked for Clarence's forwarding address. *His love for her must never be allowed to grow cold.*

CHAPTER 13

THE BENGAL FAMINE

Calcutta, May 1943

At the onset of the monsoons, a gale battered the windows of the FAU Office in Wood Street. Rain poured down in sheets as Angus entered the room, holding a sodden newspaper.

He handed Clarence the soggy mess. 'The streets are a torrent and the basement has flooded. We'll have to dry this before we can read it.'

Clarence relieved him of the papers. Painstakingly, he peeled off each one and laid them out on the carpet. Falling on his knees, he scanned the headlines and read them out aloud: *Gusts of wind tear down trees. Tidal waves break Hooghly River banks. Rice fields flood. Seawater flows into dams.*

'Well. Well. Get ready for emergencies, lads,' Angus said. 'We may soon be back on ambulance duties doing the job we've been trained for.'

By the middle of 1943, famine gripped the State of Bengal. The starving population trudged to urban centres, clamouring for aid. On hearing the news, Clarence joined Angus, Albert and Alex—a senior member of the FAU—hoping to bring some relief to the starving people. They took a taxi to the docks where they shoved their way through the crowds toward the jetty and boarded a launch with medical supplies for the sick.

Fort William appeared forbidding from the upper deck. Clarence recalled going to the fort for their papers and passports when they had first arrived. How soon he had settled into the routine of life in India!

The launch sped down the Hooghly River. It had broken its banks, flooding the low-lying fields and villages. Thick as a chocolate pudding mix, the vast expanse of muddy water swirled southwards. Timber from houses and factories demolished by the floods, swept down with the current.

Families had taken shelter on their roofs but even these could be inundated if the water continued to rise. People shouted and clasped their hands, begging for succour. With a little toot of the horn in acknowledgement, the launch swept past. Stocked as they were with essentials, there was no room for anything or anyone else.

Clarence clutched the rails. An ache rose in his throat as he realised he was powerless to help. Corpses of cattle and men drifted toward the ocean, with flocks of vultures perched on the bodies, tearing at the carrion.

Angus screwed up his face. '*They* won't starve from the famine.'

Clarence's mind went back to his journey from Liverpool to Calcutta by sea, when bodies of his fellow countrymen had floated among the debris of torpedoed ships and gulls had feasted on their corpses.

Alex, who'd been in India longer than most of the others, showed no outward signs of emotion. 'Normally this area consists of sand dunes criss-crossed by a network of streams, and the bank is lined by sharp spikes from the mangroves but the floods have covered them.'

Everyone's head turned in unison like dancers in a ballet performance. They had never seen mangroves before. Spiky roots erupted from the river bed as they reached for air. Some still protruded from the ground like spears. *Just like the railings in England's parks and gardens before they were torn up for use as war material,* Clarence thought.

Angus raised a hand to his brows and searched the horizon. 'Where are the islands?'

'They're under water too. They flood during the monsoons. Some vanish forever.' Alex waved his hand in the direction of what looked like an island. 'The tops of the forests you now see are part of the mainland. They are infested with pythons, wild hogs and crocodiles.'

Angus leaned forward on the handrail. 'Bloody nice place to be in!'

'Are there any bigger game?' Albert asked, gazing at the forest.

'Oh yes. You also get Bengal tigers, leopards and rhinoceros.' Alex handed his binoculars to Albert, but Angus snatched them from him and trained the binoculars upriver. He failed to see any signs of wildlife.

Albert waited his turn patiently and was rewarded by the sight of a rhino.

Unlike his two friends, Clarence had never been big on game hunting, but he caught their excitement. He, too, would like to go in search for them and do some shooting—*not with a gun but a camera!* A feeling of guilt stole over him as his thoughts returned to the object of their expedition. *This was not a pleasure trip. They were on a mercy mission.*

Further downstream, the Friends Ambulance Unit stopped at an abandoned rajah's palace, intending to use it as a temporary base. The stench of rotting corpses drenched the air. As soon as they landed, packs of baboons swung on the bamboos and jeered. Jackals fought over dead bodies, snarling and tearing them with their yellow fangs.

Contrastingly, brilliant mauve water lilies covered peaceful pools. Red and purple orchids festooned the higher branches of trees. A red jungle fowl fluttered past. Parakeets squawked, and brightly feathered kingfishers swooped on their prey. How could they survive amid such horror?

Shady palms dotted the landscape. Clarence eyed the coconuts clustered at their tops. Would one of them fall and crack his skull?

They hurried on and he stumbled over something, disturbing a swarm of flies. A dying man had crawled to the water's edge to slake his thirst. Now bloated, the corpse lay face down by the pool.

The sound of retching reached Clarence. Albert had his hand against a tree and was buckled over, heaving as he vomited. Even before his stream of sour food landed, flies droned towards it. The chums pretended not to notice him and stepped into the palace, looking around cautiously, as though afraid of whatever lay within. The rajah had left, taking his treasures and retinue of servants, leaving the villagers to starve. Clarence had seen death during the London Blitz, but now he struggled to come to terms with rich rajahs on one hand and gruelling poverty on the other. *What a city of contrasts Calcutta was!*

They did their best for the hungry with whatever supplies they carried—medicines and cans of food from their stores, which had been earmarked for China. As the crisis mounted, the government of Bengal started a Central Relief Fund, handing out clothing, blankets and free meals. Other organisations sent in tins of powdered milk for the children.

Feeding the starving hordes proved a difficult task. Each religious group and caste had its own rigid laws. Moslems would spit on the ground and curse if offered a tin of pork sausages; Hindus held up their hands in horror when given corned beef. The former regarded the pig as an unclean animal, and the latter worshipped cattle as gods.

On weary legs and aching feet, Clarence and his companions travelled from village to village. At times they managed to hitch a ride on a bullock cart. By the spring their stores were nearly depleted and they considered calling off all relief work, but Britain's convoys, carrying grain from South America for the starving, slipped through enemy submarines.

Reinforced by food supplies, Clarence went by car, bicycle or on foot helping villagers. Despite bouts of diarrhoea and abdominal pain, he staggered around, trying his best to keep up with the others. Every joint in his body—especially his ankles, knees and elbows—cried out in agony. He longed for rest as the long, aching days crept by.

At first, everyone thought he was suffering from extreme fatigue, but when he developed a sudden rise in temperature, arrangements were made for a nurse to accompany Clarence back to Calcutta. A wave of guilt swept over him at the thought of deserting his companions but they ignored his protests.

Gratefully, Clarence sank back on the clean white hospital bed. The rain tree outside his room was dotted with pink and white flowers. The breeze drifted in, bringing the sweet perfume of the frangipani flowers that covered the temple tree, as it was called in Bengal. From his window he could see the jacaranda trees swathed in blue, and the long drooping stems of the neem covered in tiny white stars. He lost count of the days, dreaming of spring in England when the snowdrops and crocuses thrust their heads through the ground.

He recovered consciousness in the summer when the scent of roses was heavy in the air from the bushes directly outside his window.

A rash covered his arms and legs, so he examined the red patches.

A figure in white moved slowly to his bedside and smiled. 'Looks like prickly heat but it's the aftermath of your fever.'

A few days later, Clarence regained his appetite. The sluggishness, however, remained for months.

He was granted rest and recuperation leave as soon as he recovered sufficient strength to walk without aid. He had often dreamed of being a missionary, so he chose to spend some of his time visiting mission stations. He wanted his spirituality to have deep foundations in solid rock and enable the power of Christ to change his base nature to a more spiritual one. From the age of fourteen Clarence had struggled to conquer his faults and often had to remind himself of the words that had been pointed out to him by one of the Church Elders: *People with a hot temper do foolish things; wiser men remain calm* (Proverbs 14:17).

He reflected that his quarrel with Mary was only one example of his short fuse.

CHAPTER 14

THE MISSION STATIONS

Calcutta, September 1943

After his bout of dengue fever, the FAU sent Clarence on leave to recuperate. He immediately wrote to Jack Christie, an English pastor, requesting permission to visit some mission stations under his jurisdiction. Now was his chance to experience life as a missionary.

Jack wrote back. 'You're most welcome to stay with me. I'll take you along when I visit my parishioners. Just let me know when you'll arrive and I'll meet you at the station.'

Chris Barber drove Clarence to Calcutta station in time to catch the train for Bihar. 'Have a good holiday and don't work too hard,' he said, shaking hands.

As the train pulled out of the station, Clarence flipped the rail tickets from the FAU against his knees, his heart beating with excitement.

Jack was true to his word and Clarence spotted him straight away as he disembarked from the train. A short walk brought them to his brick bungalow. A servant brought a pail of hot water and Clarence rinsed himself in a tin bath. He'd taken the precious liquid for granted all his life, but here, it had to be carted from a nearby well and stored in earthenware jars.

Refreshed after his bath, he stepped outdoors, where bougainvillea grew in a profusion of colours.

Four ladies were walking in the garden and the eldest one approached him. 'Welcome. I am Mrs Banerjee. These are my co-workers.'

The other three raised their folded hands to their forehead and bowed.

'Welcome, sir.' In unison they flung their *saris* over their shoulders.

Clarence raised his hat. 'Thank you.'

Mrs Banerjee then threw questions at him, gesticulating with hand and head movements.

Clarence found it wearisome to keep up with her chatter and was delighted when Jack rescued him from their incessant talking.

The next day after breakfast, Jack and Clarence cycled out to look at a new rest house for visitors. They rode on until they came to a river approximately three quarters of a mile wide, in which a guide strode, prodding the water with a long bamboo to judge its depth. A stream of people followed him.

The muddy waters flowed sluggishly. Small branches floated along, sometimes getting entangled with creepers that hung precariously from the banks. Bullock carts plunged through the ford. An elephant brought up the rear, swishing its trunk to hose down the dust on its head and shoulders while it waded through the water.

Jack hired a cart to carry their bicycles across. They climbed into the wooden wagon and joined the procession of travellers. Water splashed over the sides, but they crossed safely and continued on their cycles until they arrived at the rest house.

Lime plaster covered the mud and brick building, which had an earthen floor like most village homes. The two men threw themselves upon a floor mattress and, in spite of the hardness of his bed and his aching muscles, Clarence fell asleep within a few minutes.

The following day being Sunday, Jack Christie took the service. The church was a fair-sized brick-and-tile building. Sun streamed down from a stained glass window above the pulpit, throwing chequered colours on the worshippers, who knelt at the pews. The men dressed in clean white *dhotis* and the women in colourful *saris*. Like most village churches, people sat on the floor, with a row of chairs at the back for visiting missionaries. Clarence chose a seat near the entrance to get the breeze.

Jack spoke in the native dialect and only occasionally threw in a word or two in English, so Clarence couldn't understand the sermon. Contemplating the reflections of the stained glass above, his mind wandered off to Nottingham. *Mary, even now, could be sitting in church, praying for my welfare. How would she like being a missionary's wife? Well, I'll withhold my judgement of the missions until the end of my visit.*

He wrenched his thoughts back to the present as a slight breeze ruffled the leaves outside the church, stirring up the odour of human sweat and coconut oil that the Indians used for their hair. He shifted his posture on the hard seat, wondering whether the pews housed any bugs.

On Monday, Jack and Clarence set out for another mission. Jack walked ahead, swinging his arms in a steady rhythm. They followed field paths through jungle-covered hills and dry riverbeds embedded with twisted tree trunks until they came to a hamlet. An hour's walk brought them to the hospital, administrative buildings and houses for government servants, all built of local stone. The bungalow was also built of the same material.

The stars were already beginning to peep by the time Jack and Clarence arrived, but they stayed up late, talking to their hosts.

After returning to Jack's house, Clarence and Jack cycled on the Lathar-Ranchi Road through a village of mud-brick houses, before turning off into the winding jungle track.

'You are likely to come across monkeys, tigers and bears at nights,' Jack said, as they rode. 'We saw a young bear cub the other day. The mother must have been captured by natives, who train the animals to dance.'

Clarence followed, listening to the sounds of the jungle. The hairs on the nape of his neck rose at every sound.

'Don't worry,' Jack said, as though reading his thoughts. 'Bears rarely attack humans unless threatened. Tigers, too, are usually a threat at nights only.'

They trudged on in silence, pushing their bikes along as they forded a small stream with moss-covered rocks.

Jack stopped midstream, and indicated some broken branches among the bushes on the right bank. 'I found four headless bodies at this spot not long ago.'

Clarence shook, and lifting his eyes from the river bed, nearly lost his balance. 'Do head-hunters live here?'

'No. Head-hunters reside on the Burmese border. They shrink the heads of their victims and decorate their huts with them. Robbers decapitated these bodies and buried their heads elsewhere to prevent identification.'

Jack paused while negotiating a particularly demanding area. 'They were killed pending a lawsuit with a local landlord, whom locals believe is responsible for the murder.'

Was Jack speaking of his Christian parishioners or the Hindu villagers who formed the majority of the population? Clarence knew that the missionaries were working hard to convert the natives to Christianity. He didn't allow his mind to dwell on the subject for long but remained alert to every sound in the jungle. He started whenever a twig snapped. *Was an animal or a thug stalking them?* His muscles tensed.

After a safe crossing, they came to a stretch of smooth, grassy bank. An ideal spot to stop—secluded and undisturbed. Hot and tired, they settled down to enjoy a lunch of corned beef sandwiches, followed by a dessert of guava cheese.

They visited the village headman's house after their meal. On their arrival, the whole family came out to greet them. A woman brought out a brass bowl of water, washed their hands and knelt down.

She attempted to remove Jack's shoes but he waved her off. 'No, madam. I cannot permit you to perform such a menial task,' he said.

'At least allow me to place garlands around your ankles,' their hostess said.

She performed the same welcoming ceremony for Clarence before brewing tea in a large earthen-ware pot and serving the beverage in brass bowls.

Jack lost no time in taking Clarence to yet another mission the following day. Judging by the absence of pews and bamboo mats to cover the floor of the church, Clarence realised it was rather an impoverished parish.

Their host invited them to join in the midday meal of rice, dhal, spinach and fried potato cakes. Everyone ate with their fingers, Indian style. Clarence swayed, finding it difficult to sit on his haunches. He longed for a chair. Like his hosts, he scooped up the food, pushing it into his mouth with his thumb, but the effort was too great. He lost his balance and nearly overturned his plate of food. He saved the contents from spilling but his juggling act made him fall against his neighbour.

'Sorry!' His face turned a bright red.

The man next to him shook his head sideways, native style. 'My humble apologies, sir. I think you need something to sit on.' He rose and fetched a low stool for Clarence, who finished his meal in silence.

That night, they slept on the floor again but their hostess had placed freshly washed linen, cotton blankets and two mattresses on a bamboo mat. The sheets smelled of Sunlight soap.

A few days later, Clarence set off to the next mission station with Dorrie, Jack's wife. Jack remained behind as he had to report the theft of rice on some of the plantations to the police. They rode down to the bus stop on their bicycles. The road was rough and washed away by floods in some places, forcing the driver to detour through a harvested paddy field.

The jalopy forded two rivers, clattered down steep banks into sandy streambeds and strained up the slopes in low gear.

They arrived at half past seven. Clarence lowered his aching body from the bus and checked in at a bungalow. Dorrie prepared supper for them and before leaving to spend the night with an Indian nurse she knew, she produced a tin of insect repellent and dusted his bed as an insurance against bugs. As a result, Clarence awoke refreshed the next morning.

Dorrie returned and greeted him without her usual smile, her eyes swollen from lack of sleep. 'The bed swarmed with bugs,' she said. 'I didn't want to upset my hostess by using the insecticide, and passed a sleepless night scratching myself. I hope it doesn't bring on a skin infection.'

They attended church—a mud building with an earthen surface. The congregation of about twenty-five people squatted on the floor, the men in front and the women at the back. Dorrie and Clarence sat on a couple of string beds that served as seats. They listened to the hymns, which were in Hindi but sung to the old familiar tunes. During the collection, people placed little bundles of rice in the basket in lieu of church dues. Clarence recalled the Bible story of the widow's offering and recognised the similarity.

After the service, they strolled home via the fields, passing villagers harvesting grain with sickles. Dorrie kept scratching the bug bites, and Clarence was beginning to get irritated, but he checked his uncharitable thoughts. After all, she had dusted his bed with insecticide the night before. Otherwise, he, too, would now be in agony.

They were invited out to a Hindu *karhna* that evening. Everyone sat on mats in the light of hurricane lamps and ate with their fingers. Clarence, who was beginning to understand the Indian way of eating, enjoyed the meal of rice, chicken curry, spicy bean cakes and dahl. The spices transformed the meal into a symphony of taste.

After dinner, the host took him to a drumming. Three youths played on the instruments while the rest of the party sat around a fire near one of the threshing floors and sang hymns in Hindi. The drummers seemed to be in a trance as they kept up the same monotonous beat, similar to the sounds he'd heard around Hindu temples.

Did Hindus bring their customs with them when converted to Christianity? Clarence wondered but felt it impolite to ask.

They left at half past nine, but the thrum of the distant drumming swelled like a heartbeat and continued late into the night.

After a restless sleep, owing to the cold and to the bits of straw that somehow worked right through his clothes, Clarence woke early. On the way to the next mission, he caught a glimpse of the rajah's palace. Its wrought-iron gate reminded him of a nineteenth century workhouse in London. He cycled along in silence. Thoughts of home always made him withdraw into his own world— his Creator, his family and Mary.

Clarence and Dorrie rode on until they came to a river where two bullock carts were waiting to take them across. He swung their bicycles onto the cart, helped Dorrie up and clambered in. The driver prodded his bullocks with a length of bamboo and they broke into a trot before descending into the river and wading towards the opposite bank.

As they neared the other side, a stench arose and a swarm of flies buzzed around, feasting on a dead dog. Three birds with bald red heads were tearing at it with their beaks and talons. *Vultures,* Clarence thought, *feeding on carrion.* 'Repulsive creatures,' he muttered out loud.

His mind strayed to the briefness of life and the eternity of death. In war, lives were cut short.

They returned to Jack and Dorrie's place in time for dinner. Jack met them, looking relaxed and happy. 'I suggest we have an early night as we'll be off early tomorrow on your final tour of my parish.'

At six in the morning, Jack woke Clarence from a deep sleep as he needed to visit a village twelve miles away and had to make an early start. Before leaving, Jack sent a man to engage a *charpoy* and four coolies. They were off within an hour.

On their arrival at a river, the men waited on them, holding a low Indian cot with strong white cotton tapes interlacing to form a mat nailed to the frame.

'Why do we need beds?' Clarence asked. 'Are we going to camp here?' He thought of the wild beasts that would come to drink water during the night and shuddered.

Jack smiled. 'Please get up on the bed and leave the rest to the natives.'

A bearer placed Clarence's bicycle on the bed and Clarence clambered on. He sat cross-legged, waiting for the next move.

Jack nodded to the bearers, who picked it up and placed each corner upon their shoulders. The *charpoy* leaned precariously on the uneven riverbed but Clarence hung on until they reached the opposite bank. The coolies then returned for Jack.

Clarence wished he had brought along his Brownie camera. *What a remarkable photograph it would have made!*

After collecting their bikes, they turned off the road and followed rough jungle paths. Dust, several inches deep, covered the worn tracks. Ruts had weathered the path and large boulders blocked the way. Clarence found the riding difficult, so they dismounted and wheeled their bicycles along while Jack pointed out the landmarks.

'It's important to recognise these signs in case you may stray off the path and get lost,' he explained.

They visited all the Christians in the area, getting the same reception wherever they went. Finally, they returned for a well-earned rest and a meal of rice and hot curry, two and a half hours later.

That night Clarence lay awake for a long time. The first part of his leave was over. He had witnessed sights he would never have been able to conjure up even in his dreams. In spirit, he was willing to put up with such hardships but his body was weak. He realised he couldn't dedicate his entire life to such work and he knew he'd sooner or later succumb to some tropical disease. Even now, his stomach squealed in protest at the hot curries, although he'd tried his utmost to avoid whatever was likely to cause an upset.

He longed for home cooking. Visions of his mother's delicious roasts and the taste of chocolate with its smooth velvety touch and imitable flavour rose before him.

No. The food in India would stop him from ever being a missionary in this vast continent that desperately needed to receive God's message. He could put up with the inconvenience—the heat, the lack of water, the bugs, the wild animals and long treks through the jungle to visit his parishioners. That would be fine, but his weak stomach could not tolerate the food. Hadn't his flight to China been put off because of his recurring diarrhoea?

He decided to leave the apostolic work in India to those stronger in health than himself.

CHAPTER 15

THE TAJ & CHRISTMAS

Northern India, November 1943

Clarence packed his portmanteau for the next leg of his journey. At the railway station he produced his passport and, as a member of the FAU, he obtained a berth in a 'Military Only' compartment. Two RAF and two army personnel were also in the carriage but they kept to themselves.

On his arrival at Delhi, to his surprise, Angus and Albert were waiting for him outside the yellow sandstone hotel.

'We've been given leave as well as the cost of our tour, meals and accommodation,' Angus said, putting out his hand. 'We cadged a flight with some air force boys who were coming over.'

Clarence beamed and extended his hand. 'So glad to see you again … What's it like down at Cal?'

'Hotter than cinders,' Angus answered, shaking hands with him.

As they entered the hotel, the bellboy grabbed their portmanteaus and escorted them to their rooms. After receiving his tip, he left with a *salaam* and a bow.

Arising early, the trio boarded a bus crowded with soldiers on leave, but Angus elbowed his way through to the back where they managed to get seats. The weather was cool and dry in November and to avoid potholes, the driver swerved on the dust-covered roads. They passed a lake with an imposing building in the centre.

'How do they build such a solid structure in the middle of the water?' Clarence asked the guide.

The man waggled his head from side to side. 'Easy, sir. When it dried up in the dry season they built the foundation above the waterline. Once the rains were over, they finished the construction.'

Clarence imagined teams of labourers slaving in the heat of summer for a mere pittance and his heart went out to them.

The following day they left for Agra. They waited in the hotel lounge for the bus to the Agra Fort—also known as the Red Fort because of the colour of the sandstone used in its construction. Once there, the guide showed them a glimpse of the Taj Mahal in the distance. The radiant white marble gleamed on the horizon.

While Clarence gazed at the imposing mausoleum, he felt a sudden tug at his arm. Surprised, he glanced down and smiled. A monkey stood next to him. Its head leaned to one side and its large brown eyes pleaded for a handout.

Clarence reached in his bag and held out a banana, which it snatched before it disappeared.

Within a few minutes, a red-faced lieutenant was swearing at the primate as it jumped up and down, its yellow fangs bared; the officer's swagger stick in its hand.

The sergeant and several Indians ran after it.

Clarence and his friends couldn't wait to witness the outcome of the chase as their guide kept beckoning them.

'So many areas within the fort are out of bounds,' Albert grumbled.

Clarence placed a hand on his young friend's arm. 'Remember that Britain has to safeguard her possessions from sabotage.'

Albert shrugged and strode on but the frown upon his face had disappeared once they boarded the bus for the Taj Mahal.

The magnificent edifice came into view at the entrance of the great archway leading to the ornamental gardens. It stood on a raised marble platform. Clarence gazed awestruck at the building, fascinated by the emperor's extravagant devotion for his wife. His heart beat fast as he thought of Mary. How could he prove himself to her? There had been an understanding between them, but he hadn't declared his love for her. With so many US and Polish troops in England at the moment, he wanted her to remain free to marry whom she chose. Besides, something could happen to him. Although safe enough here in India, once in China, the risk of dying from disease or bombs was high.

Clarence slid his hand along the smooth walls. The splendour of the Taj was marvellous in its own way, but European architecture was grand too. Both were breath-taking and awe-inspiring—each representing its respective culture.

His pulse quickened at the sight of the world-famous building but he found difficulty in understanding the stark contrast of the Taj with the poverty he'd witnessed.

Angus gave him a gentle nudge as the sightseers pressed behind them. Albert had already entered. Clarence stepped inside, surprised to find the interior of the tomb so small, with just enough space for a single file of visitors to circle around the coffin that lay in a cavity below.

They continued their sightseeing in the pink city of Jaipur. The sun shone and buildings reflected a rosy hue from their stone.

'The city has retained its pink colour ever since 1876 when it was painted to welcome the Prince of Wales,' the guide said. 'In India, pink stands for the colour of hospitality.'

After lunch, they went to the Amber Fort. On their way back their guide stopped at the red sandstone Jaipur railway station. 'The cupolas are like a woman's breast.' He held his hands out as if he were even now, cupping them. 'You must go in, *sahibs*. Inside are paintings of gorgeous women.'

Angus strode ahead, making a path for them through the crowds.

Before entering, Albert looked up and beamed. 'They do look like breasts.'

Once inside, all admired the murals.

On their way out, rickshaw *wallahs* flew at them like bats, asking, 'Where are you going *sahibs*?' When their guide waved them off, they descended upon the next likely customer.

After dropping them off at their hotel, the guide held out his hand for the inevitable *buckshee*.

With regret, they finally left for their headquarters at Calcutta. As the train chugged along, Clarence marvelled at the bizarre contrast of wealth and destitution within the subcontinent. He recalled his first trip to Calcutta across India earlier in the year. Many things had happened since then. *If it were not for the war, I'd never have left home and witnessed such splendour,* he thought.

At Calcutta station, beggars and hawkers tried to besiege them but white-gartered policemen pushed them back with their batons. One of the supplicants had bandaged her knees with rags and used wood blocks to crawl along. Her pitiful appearance tore at Clarence's heartstrings and he *had* to throw her a coin.

They hailed a cab and headed back to the hotel. On the way they passed a dance club where strains of *Alouette* drifted out through the open windows.

'People must be dancing in there with happy abandon,' Albert said. 'Wish we could join them.'

The taxi pulled up outside Wood Street and they descended, ready for a bath and a cool drink of lemon fizz.

A letter from Doug awaited Clarence at his hostel. A postmark showed it had been posted from the village of Battapaglia in Italy.

In a fever of anxiety, Clarence listened to the radio and read the papers for the latest news of the fighting in Italy. British losses in Salerno had been heavy. He nibbled at his lower lip. A layer of grief as fine as dust lay on his heart. Each day it grew heavier when his brother's mail had failed to reach him on time. Doug wrote monthly but his mail arrived at varying intervals. Sometimes several letters from him came in at the same time.

***

Italy, July 1943 to 1944

After the Allied victory in North Africa, Doug had been posted to Italy. The change from dry sandy desert to soggy wet conditions disheartened the men. They trudged through waterlogged roads, delayed by land mines and booby traps laid by the retreating German troops. Sappers worked hard clearing the mines. Engineers followed, building Bailey bridges to span the rivers. Because of the unforeseen delays, the men ran short of rations. Undeterred, those who were capable rode requisitioned horses to their supply lines, bringing them their rations.

As the advanced guard neared Scafati on the River Sarno, they mistook the rumblings of Mt Vesuvius for cannon fire and went forward cautiously. The British 10 Corps swept around Vesuvius to the Naples plains and continued north.

British losses had been heavy in Salerno but despite this, Doug wrote a cheery letter to Clarence saying that he'd served in Palestine, Egypt, Libya and Tunisia, and could now add Sicily to the list. He enjoyed the fresh fruits, vegetables and nuts, but sandflies and malaria were prevalent everywhere.

***

Back in Nottingham, Roy was called up to military service in May. His turn had come to join his brothers and fight the enemy. He was delighted to at last be in the army. Roy realised that the stress of war had hastened his mother's early demise. Now he was free to avenge her death. His father was mourning his recent loss, and Eva had never been much company for Roy. They had always been quarrelling.

He thought of Clarence. He couldn't understand his stance on war, but he was still proud of the way he'd stood up to everyone and expressed his views at court.

***

During the mild Indian winter from December to January, Clarence, Angus and Albert went for strolls on the *Maidan*. Police tore down 'Quit India' placards in the main streets and replaced them by 'V for victory' slogans, but the 'Quit India' signs still plastered walls of buildings in the backstreets where the British rarely frequented.

Calcutta papers like *The Statesman* and *The Hindustan Star* informed Clarence of battles in Europe and Africa. His mind returned to England where planes had roared across the sky and the hum of a convoy of transport vehicles was interspersed with the tramp of marching feet.

In December shops became crowded. Rickshaws jammed the streets, carrying women on shopping sprees. Stallholders, extolling their wares, vied with the quacking of ducks and the flapping of wings in the poultry stalls. The three chums jostled among the crowds with their hands in their pockets to safeguard their money from pickpockets. They feasted their eyes on mounds of candied peel, preserved pumpkins, sugared cherries and wrinkled raisins set out on tables.

After each had bought a rich fruitcake to send back to their families in Britain, they returned to their quarters for a siesta. The noise and haggling had been almost too much for Clarence's sensitive nerves, but he drifted off to sleep and dreamed of home.

The week before Christmas, Chris Barber said, 'Calcutta has a Pickwickian zest for Christmas. I'll take you to the bakeries where local bakers bake Christmas cakes in clay ovens. The mince pies here are as good as the ones back home.'

The aroma of baking wafted to them as they approached the shops. Clarence hoped the cake he had posted out would reach his family in time. He imagined their last gathering. The sounds of hawkers became subdued as he daydreamed of roast duck and plum pudding back home. He pictured his mother walking into the dining room with the steaming pudding and her expectant face as she paused for her husband's verdict. His saw his father giving thanks to the Lord, then standing poised, knife in hand, while all waited patiently in their paper party hats.

'Delicious as usual,' he had always said.

Clarence moistened his lips and sighed as he returned to the present.

Chris nudged him. 'The FAU is treating all new-comers to high tea at Flury's. By the time we've finished, the carollers will be on the streets. We'll have a Dickensian Christmas.'

Flury's shop window displayed mince pies, chocolate cones, yule logs and cakes covered by snow white icing, decorated with holly, miniature reindeer and Santas. They filled Clarence with nostalgia.

'It's the custom here for Christians to keep open house all day,' Chris said. 'Friends drop in to exchange greetings, have a slice of cake and a glass of port or sherry. I'll take you to meet an acquaintance tomorrow morning.'

'Where will we be having dinner?' Albert asked.

'Ah,' Chris replied, putting his finger on the side of his nose. 'You'll know soon enough.'

They entered Flury's and a waiter led them to the table. A delicious array of finger sandwiches, sweet pastries, freshly baked scones with jelly and Cornish clotted cream, and slices of cake were served in a three-tiered plate.

Chris rubbed his hands. 'Help yourselves, chums.'

Angus took in the silverware and the crystal chandeliers. 'This rivals the Ritz.'

Clarence nodded. 'The colonies are much better off than we are back home,' he said, reaching out for a slice of chocolate cake.

They all tucked in, leaving with appetites sated.

Bands of carol singers crowded the streets, bringing to mind days long gone. It had been some time since Clarence had experienced such a joyful exhibition of the Christmas season. Thrilled to the core, they returned home around half past eight and retired after a cup of cocoa.

On Christmas morning, Chris took the three friends visiting as he had promised. 'I'd like you to see how an Anglo-Indian family celebrates Christmas,' he said.

Their hostess met them at the door. After greeting them heartily, she led them into the lounge. It had a traditional Christmas tree, complete with a nativity scene underneath. After a few minutes, she brought out two crystal decanters and asked, 'Port or sherry?'

A servant entered, carrying a tray laden with cake, nuts and *dohl dohl*. The latter was made from black gluten rice, coconut milk and sugar.

Within half an hour, more guests arrived and Chis thanked his host and hostess for their hospitality before leaving.

Around midday they had a Christmas dinner with turkey and plum pudding at the Grand Hotel. Everyone wore paper party caps and Chris dressed as Santa, handing out envelopes containing cheques from the Friends Ambulance Unit.

Clarence could hardly believe that a country managed to celebrate so well with a war raging all round them. *Dear God, please grant those at home a joyous Christmas too,* he prayed, *and please keep Doug and Roy safe.*

At the end of the festive season, Clarence continued his studies in Chinese language and culture. While packaging parcels for the China unit, he kept repeating the numbers in Chinese until he knew them by heart.

In mid-1944, Clarence finally received his orders for China. A bubble of excitement rose to his throat. Now he'd be able to see what life in the Far East was like.

CHAPTER 16

YUNNAN

India, July 1944

They had stopped at Dinjan where the flight captain received the latest weather reports. 'Be ready to bail out when I tell you,' he warned. 'A trail of aluminium wreckage marks the route all the way from Assam to Kunming, but there are Gurkhas on the ground to rescue survivors so you won't get lost.'

Before taking off from the airport, he handed each passenger a folded brown receptacle and grinned, giving the impression they were off for a joy ride. 'Just in case you need it.'

To make room for more passengers, mechanics had removed the gun, plugging the holes left by the screws. One of the plugs had fallen off, letting a stream of cool air into the cabin. The weather had been hot and the plane was like an oven when they boarded, and then the fresh air had been a welcome relief from the heat. But now the temperature plummeted.

Clarence had not been over-enthusiastic about flying under such appalling conditions, but he had waited a long time to get into China and no obstacle could deter him. Despite his windcheater and the thick woollen sweater his mother had knitted, the cold penetrated his bones. His breath came in short gasps. *How much worse the poor bloke sitting by the gunport must be!*

In spite of a thick haze covering the plains and the foothills below, Clarence caught glimpses of forest, rivers and steep valleys. He glanced down, dazzled by a glint of light through a break in the clouds, and spotted a wrecked plane partially hidden by the dense foliage. Clarence realised that flying over the Hump involved the risk of crashing, but it was the only remaining route after Japan had cut off the Burma Road to China. He had faced danger before. He thought of London. By the grace of God he'd come through unscathed.

The wind howled, its breath like a knife thrust. At 17,000 feet, the two pilots sealed off the flight deck and turned on the oxygen in the cockpit, as they needed clear heads to navigate through this area of storms, snow-capped peaks and unpredictable wind across the low saddle of the Himalayas.

A series of jolts buffeted the plane above the dense layers of clouds.

'The plume of Everest,' the flight captain shouted over the noise of the engine.

Violent gusts of wind from the crest of Everest drove the snow high into the air, which whirled upwards before falling, forever tying itself in knots and undoing them—a sight Clarence would never forget. A thrill of fear shot through him as he gazed at the sharp peaks.

Light-headed from the high altitude, Clarence kept his food down by sheer will power, determined not to use the paper bag.

The nausea passed as they commenced flying level with the crests. With a sigh of satisfaction, he glanced at his fellow travellers. The passenger by the gunport was in a foetal position, showing signs of asphyxiation from the lack of oxygen. Only the seat belt prevented him from falling.

They skimmed over the mountains. Clarence gazed down from thousands of feet of space and caught his first glimpse of China. Every inch of the countryside was under heavy cultivation. Rectangular patches of vivid red, green, white, and purple fields followed the contours of the hills, where a couple of monasteries were precariously perched on the edges.

The plane began its descent and circled Kunming, a small dot on the atlas in southwest China. The city sprawled out near a large lake, making a wonderful picture in the crystal-clear air and dazzling sun.

'Nearly there,' the pilot shouted, as the plane dipped towards the runway.

Clarence relaxed. Due to the lack of oxygen, along with the cold of a non-pressurised cabin, the trip from Assam had seemed much longer than three hours.

Bill Skurr, with whom Clarence had travelled on board the *SS Strategist* to India, met them at the airport. He shook hands with a firm grip, glancing at everyone's red noses. 'Hope the flight was not too arduous.'

Bill's cheery face made Clarence think of his days in London during the Blitz when he had worked with his brother, Jack. Both were Quakers, good-looking, with youthful faces.

'How different this part of the world is,' Clarence said. 'Calcutta was hot and dry with the temperature no less than eighty degrees in the shade, but here it's so fresh.'

Bill glanced up at the mountains. 'The wind blows across the glaciers and keeps us cool even in summer.'

Clarence rubbed his hands and folded his arms.

Ch'en, a Chinese member of the Friends Ambulance Unit, gave two quick bows and held out his right palm, at the same time holding his forearm with the other. His hand was warm, but his clasp loose.

'Is Kunming a large city?' one of the passengers asked.

'The population has swelled to nearly three hundred thousand, with refugees from all over. Many British, American and Free French are here too,' Bill answered, before stepping on the accelerator and driving towards their quarters.

Cypress-covered hills, shrouded in mist, stretched on both sides of the road from the airport.

'Yunnan has half of China's plant and animal species,' Bill said.

He drove via the massive city gates into Kunming and halted the truck in front of the hostel where they all spilled out, dirty and dishevelled. Clarence ran his fingers through his hair in an attempt to tidy himself.

Ch'en beckoned to the passengers who had been posted to medical teams and led them off.

Bill rubbed his smoothly shaven square jaw and looked at Clarence. 'I'll take you to your quarters straight away. You'll feel better after a hot shower and something to eat.'

He climbed a set of stairs along a draughty corridor and Clarence followed, still a bit unsteady on his feet from the flight. Bill unlocked a door two rooms from the end and turned on the lights. A lamp with a naked electric bulb stood on a desk against a wall. An inbuilt wardrobe, with a sliding panel, occupied the space at the foot of a camp bed.

'Dinner will be served in an hour. Plenty of time to freshen up,' Bill said. 'See you in the morning.'

Clarence sat on the bed, which sagged alarmingly. He jumped up and started unpacking—a difficult feat in such a squashed space. His next thought was to have a piping-hot shower. He let the water sluice over every inch of his body, then stepped out of the cubicle, tingling and alert.

After changing into something fresh, hunger and curiosity drove him to the dining room. The place was crowded with FAU drivers from outlying stations, but Clarence did not recognise anyone. Too tired for small talk, he took up a tray and walked down the line, collected the *chow*, and headed for a seat in the corner. He removed the cover from his dish—roast meat, peas, carrots and mashed potatoes, with two slices of bread and butter.

Scarcely had he taken his first bite when the man nearest to him moved over and sat beside him. 'Hello, I'm Jim. Off to Kutsing tomorrow.'

Clarence put out his hand. 'Clarence.'

Two other men joined them.

'Stanley and Gray, our best mechanics.' Jim indicated each with a wave of his arm.

Gray nodded, placed his food on the table and shook hands. 'We've been expecting you. Your chum, Parry Davies, works on the diesel team.'

'How's Parry?' Clarence asked.

'He was ill with malaria and dysentery when he first arrived, but he's fine now.'

'Not quite,' Stanley put in. 'He's love sick.'

Gray frowned at Stan. 'Quit that. Let Parry tell him all about it.' He glanced at Clarence. 'You'll get the whole story when you meet him.'

With a light step, Clarence strode to the dining room for breakfast the following morning. He had folded his trousers and placed them beneath his mattress the night before so they looked well-ironed. A swift glance around told him that he had not met any of the others before.

After a hearty meal, he reported to the office, which Bill also used as a bedroom. Above his bed was a map of Yunnan and its neighbouring states with supply routes marked in red.

The passenger who had been sitting by the gunport in the plane was waiting for instructions. His colour had returned and he was breathing freely now.

'I'll be with you in a minute,' Bill said to Clarence, rifling through a heap of documents on his desk. He handed some papers to the other man, shook hands with him and turned his attention to Clarence. 'Have a fag.'

'Thanks, I don't smoke.'

Bill slid open his drawer and dropped the packet of cigarettes in, then settled back in his chair. 'Let me fill you in about things here. Each of us receives an equal amount of pocket money. Our slogan is, *Go anywhere. Do anything.* We work in remote areas where bandits operate. Our trucks bear the Red Triangle, the Chinese equivalent of the Red Cross, and we transport medical supplies to our surgical teams.

'When we first set up the FAU here we used a warehouse in a shaded cobbled alley off one of the main roads as the office. An old hotel served as training quarters for eight Chinese recruits.'

Filled with excitement, he leaned forward. 'As soon as men and supplies arrived by ship at the Rangoon docks, our convoys went down the Burma Road, returning with as much petrol as possible before the Japanese captured the oil wells.'

Bill paused before resuming. 'I'm not sure if you already know, but just before Rangoon fell in 1942, Peter Tennant rolled out of the city with a convoy of seven trucks. The civilian population had already evacuated by then. Peter and his men pressed on until they reached the safety of Kunming. Within two days, the Japs had cut the Burma Road. Now, the only route into Yunnan is via Assam. That's why you chaps had to come over the Hump.'

Clarence knew all this already, and was more concerned with what things were like at present. 'What condition are the roads in?' he asked. 'Anything like the ones in India?'

Bill smiled. 'Although the scenery is magnificent, the roads are appalling. Vehicles wear out rapidly. Because of the scarcity of petrol, we've resorted to using charcoal to run our trucks. Have to break it into small pieces this size.' He made a little circle with his thumb and forefinger. 'The charcoal turns into gas.'

Clarence whistled. 'That would take an awful long time.'

'We have to clean the trucks every day.' Bill paused, watching the effect of his words.

Clarence scratched his head. 'Once started, do they work well?'

'Charcoal burners are highly temperamental. A trip scheduled for twenty-four hours could take a fortnight. Our charcoal trucks run from Kunming to Kutsing—about seventy-five miles.'

'I suppose you have to carry enough food for several days, if you can never tell how long a trip will take.'

'We receive the usual army rations, but whenever necessary, we live off the country and sleep anywhere. Our teams are multinational. The Chinese exist on fried rice and chew watermelon seeds between meals. They're quite tasty and very rich in protein.'

'Will I be part of a team?' Clarence asked, anxious to know what his duties would entail.

'Yes, sooner or later,' Bill replied, slapping Clarence on the back. 'Just relax and have a look around. After lunch, I'll take you to your office.'

Clarence had a hurried lunch, then he reported to Bill, who took him along the narrow corridor and down the stairs. The clatter of plates and cutlery reached him. They stepped out into the sunshine and a sour stench arose as the kitchen-help emptied a pail of slops into a bin. A concrete path led to the building where Clarence was to handle supplies. The leaves on a single sycamore tree nearby shimmered slightly in the breeze.

The warehouse was a metal shed with an arched corrugated iron roof that stretched to the ground and served as walls. Clarence ran his hand over the curved surface. 'What a novel idea.'

'You'll come across many Nissan huts over here. The pre-fabricated structures look like half-buried cans and serve as barracks and mess halls. They're strong and serviceable, though rather hot in summer.'

Clarence glanced at the stores piled up nearly to the roof, while Bill continued. 'Your job will be to receive and despatch goods. Planes fly in supplies and we truck them to Chinese strongholds throughout the country. You're in charge now. Here are the keys to the warehouse.' He jangled them and strode off with a smile, as if glad to find someone competent to handle the job.

Over the next few days, Clarence slipped into the routine without any difficulty, but it was boring and monotonous. *Back into harness. Same thing as at Calcutta.* He had done it all before. He sat with his elbows on his knees, his hands gripped together until his knuckles grew white. Is this why he had come to China?

He ached to explore the country.

A month later, Bill came in, waving a piece of paper in his hand. 'It's arrived. Look what I have.'

'What's that?' Clarence asked.

'Your provisional licence. I know you'd like a change, so I've got a temporary driving permit for you.'

Clarence let out a 'Hurrah!' Maybe he would get to meet up with his friend, Parry Davies.

Within only a few months he obtained his full driver's licence, qualifying him to drive supply trucks to remote areas. He had driven ambulances in England, but driving a coal-driven truck through mountainous roads was different.

At dinner, some weeks later, Bill told him to see him at his office in the morning. What did that mean? Maybe a transfer to a remote area in the hills. Perhaps he'd get to know more of the country and meet the long-suffering Chinese.

CHAPTER 17

KUTSING

Yunnan, September 1944

Clarence knocked at Bill's door after a breakfast of sausages and eggs followed by toast and mulberry jam—so unlike the rations in England.

'Sit down.' Bill stretched back in his chair and clasped his hands behind his head. He opened his mouth to say something, but the phone rang, and he picked up the receiver. 'I'll send them at the first opportunity,' he said, and hung up.

He studied Clarence. 'Ready to drive up some supplies to Kutsing?'

Clarence's face broke into a broad grin.

'A load of charcoal produces enough gas to travel a hundred miles, sufficient to take you to Kutsing and back. The Kunming-Kutsing run is hilly, but not as rough or steep as other sections further inland.'

Clarence rose from his seat. 'Thanks. I'll get ready for the trip.'

'Hold on,' Bill said. 'Your mechanic will see to everything, but there are a few things you need to know.'

Clarence sat down again and listened to what his superior officer had to say. He could scarcely restrain his eagerness to commence his journey.

'Never leave your truck unattended,' Bill warned. 'Cars left on their own are fair game to thieves. They carry away all moveable parts and sell them in the junk market. The hostel at Kunming has to provide long distance truck drivers with food, and have their washing done. The staff there are constantly on the go, so at times, differences of opinion arise. Be ready for the odd argument.'

Without thinking, Clarence echoed the words his mother used to say to them. 'That's life, isn't it? The important thing is to respect each other's opinions.'

He headed out with a light heart, excited to be doing something different, conscious of the responsibility given to him.

It didn't take John, the Chinese mechanic, long to prepare for the trip. In the car yard, a dirty soot-covered truck was waiting for Clarence. He drove the charcoal-fired vehicle through the mountains and windy plateau, lurching over potholes. Keeping his eyes glued to the road, he only raised them occasionally to glance at the clusters of white, pink or lavender rhododendrons on the hillsides. The snaking narrow road wound lazily at first, then shot up to the summit. John sat beside Clarence, but rarely spoke, realising he needed every effort to focus on the driving. Soon the charcoal dust covered their clothes, skin and hair. Only Clarence's blue eyes showed he was not a native.

The sound of builders' handiwork reached him above the roar of the truck as he drove into Kutsing. Once parked, Clarence looked into the mirror and took out his handkerchief, attempting to wipe the grime from his face, but that only made things worse.

He let John arrange for the Chinese coolies to unload the truck and hurried towards the office. Parry had been expecting him. The stocky Welshman had lost a few pounds, but his handshake was as firm as ever.

After a long embrace, the two men broke apart, slightly embarrassed at their display of emotion, even though the war had broken down much of their traditional British reserve. After all, when they departed each morning, neither of them could be sure whether they would ever meet again.

'How are you, Parry?'

'Fine, but things here are a bit different from India.'

'Smiling oriental faces remind me of the Indians,' Clarence responded.

Parry shook his head. 'Laughter is their normal reaction to adversity.

The Chinese have little to be cheerful about. The poor merely hang on to life.' He paused, the hint of a smile twitching at the corners of his lips. 'Seen wives carrying their mates up a hill, chum?'

Clarence chortled. 'Haven't witnessed any pigtails either.'

'That's no longer practical, but I'm sure you've come across a few old Chinese women with tiny feet.'

'Must be quite painful.'

'Ask Bill how they keep them small. Hideous!' Parry hesitated. 'You're just in time for our midweek evening meeting. Like to attend or have a cuppa?'

'I'd be grateful for a cup of tea, but that can wait. Not often that I get the chance to attend a church service.'

Clarence followed him into a large room where several men were already gathered. He sank into a chair. It was refreshing to relax in peaceful surroundings, away from the constant drone of supply planes landing and taking off from Kunming.

Soon it became clear that everyone was concentrating on something deep and powerful during the silence. Occasionally Friends rose to speak as if inspired. The Elders spoke more often than others, quoting passages from the Bible.

Clarence sat still and silent, recalling his mother's readings.

After the meeting, Parry introduced him to the rest of his team. 'This is George Parsons. Any time you want some music, ask him. He used to play in Birmingham. Now carries his sax everywhere. You've met Tom Owen and Ted Cadbury at Birmingham. Drivers of the diesel team.'

Tom and George shook hands, and Ted slapped him on his back, but they had a long trip ahead and no time to stop for a chat. They slung their kit bags over their shoulders and left.

Clarence walked past the office and Elaine Conyers, the secretary, jumped up at the sight of his blackened face. She smiled, and pointed him in the direction of the washroom. Later on, she joined them for a cup of tea.

Their Chinese cook, Jim, was preparing dinner. The arrival of a guest was his time to celebrate, so he half-sung, half-muttered to himself.

Clarence put his hands behind his back. 'I believe you've been ill,' he said to Parry when they were alone.

Parry replied in his usual staccato way. 'Contracted malaria at Dibrugarh while waiting for a plane to Kunming. Treated at local hospital. Shared same room as a sergeant with dysentery. Caught it in my weakened state.'

'Is it true you're love sick, chum?'

Parry laughed. 'Grace Chiang works with us. Charming girl.'

'Is it serious?'

'Intend to marry her.'

'What do your parents think of the match?'

'Written to them. They're Methodists. Mum can't see Grace settling down in Wales.'

'What about her side of the family? How do they feel about it?'

'Live in Chungking. Friendly. Father a retired Civil Service man. Speaks excellent English. Says a mixed marriage is out of the question.'

Clarence placed a hand on his friend's shoulder. 'Can't you find someone else? No one waiting for you back home?'

'Passionate about Grace. Prettiest of the three typists. Must have her.'

Clarence shook his head. 'I don't know what to say.'

'Thanks, chum. How's Mary? Still keep in touch?'

'We write, but the post is slow, and she's not too keen on us conscientious objectors. Sometimes I go for months without any mail from home. Letters from Doug are more frequent.' He bit his lip. It had been a while since he'd heard from his brother, who'd been fighting in Italy since the conclusion of the African campaign.

He was disappointed to find no mail waiting for him, but the cleanliness of the newly built hostel and the companionship of friends appealed to him. Kutsing lay on the junction of the unit's main routes, and because of the group-living and companionship, most of the FAU regarded the place as home. The staff held regular Sunday and midweek evening meetings, developing a long lasting cohesion.

The men worked hard, but swore like troopers. At first, Clarence wanted to get away from the obscene comments that offended him, but he controlled himself, realising he was now among men who brushed with death daily and lived in the harshest conditions.

Revived and relaxed, but reluctant to leave, Clarence shook hands with Parry for a final time. 'Nice meeting you again, chum. Keep in touch and take care.'

The truck was slow to start, making moaning, sobbing sounds like the wounded during the Blitz. Thick grey smoke from the exhaust reminded Clarence of the London fog.

Once the engine warmed up, he and John climbed in. Clarence drove along the winding track through valleys, gorges and hills covered by primula, camellias and azaleas. He gazed at the clear skies, letting the vehicle run downhill at twenty miles per hour. It creaked and groaned like an arthritic old man.

Within a short time, lightning flashed and a storm broke, lashing the lorry with tons of water and turning the track into a muddy lake. His vision obscured by the blinding rain, Clarence drove straight into a pothole. Like a hippopotamus, the truck sank into the mud and wallowed. No amount of revving moved it forward. The front wheels wailed in protest.

'Stop. I get wood,' the mechanic shouted in Pidgin English.

The engine continued to moan and groan under the heavy onslaught of wind and rain. Clarence wanted to help the mechanic, but he remained in the vehicle, not daring to leave it unattended because of Bill's warning. *Dear Lord, please don't let any brigands come along while we're stranded,* he prayed. When trucks broke down on the road its occupants were often bashed and robbed. Bandits infested the hills and respected neither the Red Triangle nor the Red

Cross painted on their trucks.

Clarence drummed his fingers on the steering wheel. The sound of the storm accentuated his isolation. He had never felt lonely before, but the solitude in this vast wilderness, which he had been admiring only a short while before, overwhelmed him. There had always been a friend beside him even during the London Blitz. Fire and bombs had haunted his nights, but he never had bad dreams in the daytime. Now, the buffeting wind shook the truck until every bolt in its old body rattled; the thunder sounded like the heavy boom of guns.

A loud banging on the window woke him to reality. John had placed several branches ahead of the submerged wheel and was signalling him to rev the engine.

Clarence had left the motor idling, knowing it would take hours to restart, especially in the rain. After much revving and shoving, the truck roared out of the rut. John stood in the biting wind, while Clarence manoeuvred the vehicle back to the road.

The rain slapped Clarence's face as the mechanic opened the door to get in. Soaking wet, John removed his outer clothes and wrung them out before putting them on again with a slight shiver.

They travelled along in silence. By the time they reached Kunming, the lights were out around the town and everyone had turned in for the night. Clarence pulled into the car park and shut off the engine with a sigh of relief. Even in the darkness he saw that the truck was covered in mud from end to end. *Whoever takes care of the vehicles will spend extra time cleaning this one.*

Once inside, Clarence crept about, not wishing to disturb the others. He switched on the lights in the kitchen and put a kettle on the stove. While waiting for the water to boil, he washed and changed his clothes, humming a tune just low enough not to disturb anyone. Later, he cradled his mug of cocoa in both hands, letting its warmth flow through his body as he mulled over the events of the day.

Eventually, he turned off the lights and fell into bed, his spirit renewed, ready to tackle the oncoming weeks.

CHAPTER 18

THE FLYING TIGERS

Kunming, November 1944

'I think we'll keep you here and let you have the occasional run to Kutsing,' Bill said the next morning. 'How would that suit you?'

'Fine. Fine. Anywhere I can be of service, you know.' An intermittent trip was exactly what he needed to keep the boredom of his usual routine at bay.

'I'm taking you to the American canteen for lunch today,' Bill said. 'Meet me here at noon. We're allowed to mix freely with the aircrew and buy drinks or meals.'

Clarence guessed that Bill's talk was leading to something important. 'Thanks. It'll be good to have a Coca-Cola.'

'Don't thank me. Just don't screw up on security. Watch what you say and who you're with. Security in the canteen is not tight and you never know who may be around. One has to be guarded, especially when approaching a Frenchman.' Bill lowered his voice. 'Difficult to distinguish Vichy French from the Free French. As you are already aware, the Vichy side with the Germans.'

Clarence nodded, recalling posters in England warning people that Hitler could be listening— to not speak carelessly. Posters such as: *Tittle Tattle Lost the Battle*, *They talked*. *This happened* and *Keep mum. She's not so dumb.*

Bill introduced Clarence to the staff on duty in the cafeteria. Smoke rose in the mess as the airmen puffed on their cigarettes, lighting one after another. The place was rancid with the fumes of nicotine. Clarence was restless and he longed for a breath of fresh air, but not wanting to offend Bill, he remained seated.

Men huddled in small groups talking shop. They chewed gum, spoke loudly and appeared in high spirits. Many gathered around the coffee urns and filled their mugs or thermoses. Dark circles sagged beneath their eyes. One lot discussed a raid they had made the night before.

Thrilled at the thought of meeting the aviators, Clarence tried to eavesdrop on the conversation.

Bill leaned over. 'That's John Rossi, an ace pilot. He's stationed here. I'll introduce you to him another time. I need to fill you in before that. In the late 1930s, American General Chennault set up a base at Kunming with the old P-40 Tomahawks and flew out sorties against the Japanese. The P-40 can out-dive just about anything.'

Clarence picked at his food, still trying to catch what the men were saying.

'Some of our air fields are a mile and a half long,' Bill droned on. 'Tens of thousands of Chinese coolies helped build them. Trucks brought the workers in. Even before the wheels came to a halt, they jumped off, clutching picks and shovels. They ran all over, filling in holes and levelling the ground with a roller weighing nearly eleven thousand pounds.'

Clarence allowed his eyes to wander around the cafeteria, taking everything in. He eyed a box of confectionary that stood against the wall, on the counter, and his mouth watered. 'What's a Hershey Bar?'

'Cadbury's chocolate. Americans call them Hershey Bars.'

His weakness for chocolate getting the better of him, Clarence reached for his wallet. 'I'd like one.'

Bill rose and pushed back his chair. 'I'll take care of it.' He paid for their lunch as well as the chocolate.

'Thanks,' Clarence said as he tore open the wrapper and placed a piece of the Hershey Bar on his tongue. 'Mm.' He savoured the sweetness and let it melt in his mouth to last longer. Small extras had become a luxury to him, and he vowed that when he got back home, he wouldn't take any of them for granted.

After his visit to the canteen with Bill, Clarence often wandered in on his own. He was sometimes drawn into a story at a nearby table. He came to know some of the fighting men and gained a new respect for these airmen who risked their lives for their countrymen—for him.

One of the aircrew told Clarence, '*Time* magazine coined the nickname *Flying Tigers* for us in 1941, ever since we shot down four bombers over Yunnan in a single air battle.' He pointed out General Chennault, who lived in a modern bungalow near the airfield. 'He goes for hunting trips during a lull in the fighting.'

Clarence turned to gaze at the man whose name he often heard mentioned in the canteen. Years spent in open-cockpit planes had etched a million lines on his face.

'Chennault believes in defensive pursuit and taught us to attack enemy bomber squadrons,' the airman continued. 'Many of us have been with him in the Flying Trapeze, a precision flying team.'

Bodies of aircrew killed in action were buried in the shadow of a nearby Buddhist pagoda, not far from the aerodrome. Even in the short time he'd been in China, Clarence had attended several burial services. The ceremonies never failed to disturb him.

A strip of rough ground surrounded a double perimeter fence and protected the airport. The base had employed local labour, but spies disguised as Chinese often carried out acts of sabotage, so during loading or unloading, the Americans only permitted military or air force personnel near a plane. The FAU was the exception.

Whenever possible, Clarence helped the aircrew unload supplies. The sentry at the airfield kept a constant watch, and never failed to scrutinise his pass before letting him enter.

Kunming hummed with American aircraft. Men with crew cuts and army fatigues milled around, hastily unloading goods in case of an enemy raid. British planes rarely landed at Kunming. They were busy bombing Burma and getting ready for the push back into their former territories. An amusing story about a Wellington carrying a British general from India caught Clarence's attention at the canteen one day. The plane flew in on its way to Chungking and crashed on landing. Fortunately everyone escaped unhurt, and even its precious cargo of whiskey remained intact in the bomb chambers. That night, the general resumed his flight to Chungking with a lighter load … and a group of aircrew at Kunming were more than usually boisterous.

In place of air raid sirens, the city had one, two, or three-ball alerts hoisted aloft a tower, and people would check the number of great red balls displayed. Most of the population ignored the first two alarm signals, but when the three-ball alert went up, all scattered like mice at the scent of a cat.

Busy in the warehouse with the timeless rhythms of sorting and storing supplies, the steady drone of planes was a background to boredom. Clarence often failed to see the signals and, by the time the town shook with the vibration of enemy aircraft and the explosion of bombs, it was too late to make his way to an air raid shelter. He would then race up to the top of a hill close to his Nissen hut and watch the dogfights over the airport.

At times, in between packing supplies, Clarence drove a truck to remote areas where he shared lodging with the Chinese. The hostess invariably served a steaming bowl of *congee*, garnished with water-lily seeds and hot baked cakes stuffed with ham, onion and parsley. Nourishing and warm.

He grew to love the natives in spite of their strange ways. They insisted on his joining in their discussions. They'd sit for hours drinking tea, cracking melon seeds and eating sweets, laughing whether sad or emotional. Laughter helped them to put up with the challenge of unbeatable odds. Clarence sat through these meetings, wishing he had the time to humour them, but he was eager to get on with his job and deliver essential supplies to his mates in far off stations.

The insatiable curiosity of the Chinese drove them to comment on personal possessions and ask embarrassing questions. It made it rather difficult to know whether they were simply curious, or being paid by the Japanese to spy for them.

On one occasion, someone mentioned that a girl was going to run off with another bloke.

'How do you know this?' someone asked.

The man sipped his tea and smacked his lips before replying. 'Her sister wrote and advised her to consider well before taking such an action.' He paused. 'I deliver the mail, but always open the ones I think may be interesting.'

When delivering supplies to distant places, Clarence often bedded down on earthen floors in roadside huts. Rats would crawl over him and the night air pinched his nose with its frosty fingers. On winter nights, a slow fire burned in a hole beneath the brick-bed. The intense cold drove him to lay his bedroll on top of the warm furnace and share an oven-bed with his host, curled up in his grey army blanket.

In the mornings, his numbed fingers lit the charcoal for his lorry. He wrestled with the steering wheel on weatherworn roads and returned streaked with dust and grime, ready for a hot bath at Kunming. Life was diametrically opposite to what he had grown accustomed to at Calcutta, where he had servants, good food, a refrigerator and other modern conveniences at his disposal.

From April 1944, the city of Kweilin turned into a scene of devastation. During air raids, crowds stampeded to the hills, carrying their bedding, chopsticks and bowls. They huddled down in caves. Those nearest the entrance ran the risk of being hit by shrapnel, but they escaped the suffocating smells of unwashed bodies and clothes soiled by faeces because of diarrhoea, dysentery or fear.

Once the bombing stopped and the drone of the planes died away, they picked up their babies and their belongings and trudged back to the fields.

When Japanese troops moved towards Kweilin in November, the Flying Tigers began demolition of their airfields before retreating to Kunming. The Chinese rear guard burned crops and removed railway lines after the last trainload of their soldiers and refugees had left.

American pilots flew dead and dying troops from the front line at Kweilin to the safety of Kunming. Every two minutes, aircraft arrived, loaded with victims from the bombing raids. They landed thick and fast, pausing just long enough to refuel. Clarence always raced to the airfield in an ambulance and, putting his arm around the walking-wounded, helped them off the plane.

Often, the sickly odour of death assailed his nostrils. He sniffed. 'What's that smell?'

'I carried a load of corpses in the previous flight, but didn't have time to disinfect the aircraft before turning around,' the pilot replied.

He glanced at the wounded. 'These boys need attention. I'm off for another load as soon as I've refuelled. Back at Kweilin, they're sheltering in the caves, awaiting evacuation. General Chennault sits at the mouth of a cave, smoking his Camel cigarette and planning his next move. I'm sure he'll hit back with a vengeance.'

Whenever possible, Clarence accompanied a pilot to Kweilin, helping evacuate the wounded. On one occasion, dozens of aircraft congested the airfield, leaving little room for rescue vehicles to move in and tow them off the tarmac. Clarence jumped out and tried his best to push the craft out of the way before the next one landed. The deafening roar of aircraft, shouts of men and the smell of diesel filled the air. His heart pounded. He choked with the fumes. The plane coughed flames across its fuselage and bled smoke. The pilot fired red flares, alerting emergency crew that the aircraft contained wounded.

Enemy planes could fly in at any moment and strafe the airport.

Clarence pictured the plane bursting into flames as shots hit the fuselage. His fear of fire flared up once again, and he wanted to run off and save himself, but he exerted all his strength and pushed the plane, trying to get it off the runway. Rescuers left their vehicles and ran over to lend their weight, and ambulance vehicles chased the plane until it coasted to a stop, the propellers still wheeling.

They made it just as the next aircraft thudded down and headed towards them. The lights from the plane blinded Clarence, but he jumped clear in seconds.

Within a few days, Japan bombed Chungking and occupied eastern China. The Chinese ran short of stretchers to cart their dead and wounded, so they tore doors from their hinges to use instead.

Sometime in the spring of 1944, Parry came in to collect stores from Kunming.

The following morning, Bill gave Clarence the day off, realising that both men needed a break. 'It's a pity to be at Kunming and not go to the Stone Forest,' he said. 'We have a spare vehicle. Why not take Parry with you?'

Clarence and Parry drove out to visit the natural wonder, passing rice fields, before ascending the spruce-covered hills that rose to a height of some ninety-eight feet. Donkeys pulled carts and women wearing silver, turquoise or coral necklaces pushed trolleys of oranges on the bone-shattering roads. Others bore rice baskets attached to the end of long bamboo poles slung across their shoulders.

Clarence gasped at the sight of a woman carrying a man up a steep staircase, leading to a temple. 'I thought you'd been pulling my leg when you told me about women carrying their husbands!'

'They belong to the Pai tribe and do all the work.' Parry explained. His voice lacked the vibrancy and enthusiasm it usually held.

Clarence remained silent, knowing that, eventually, his friend would reveal his troubles to him.

About an hour's drive out of Kunming, they distinguished the weathered limestone clusters, leached white at the tips. The prehistoric seabed had been elevated over time, becoming a towering forest of stone pinnacles, arches, needles and pillars.

'Don't want to give planes or bandits an easy target,' Clarence said, as he parked the lorry at a spot partially hidden by trees.

They strolled towards the lookout in silent wonder, the fallen needles making a soft, resilient carpet beneath their heavy boots. Clarence bent down, gathered some and, crushing them between his fingers, held them to his nose. The strong smell of pine invigorated him.

A steep stone stairway twisted its way upwards. Roots of small-leaved trees entwined the rock. By the time they reached the top, both were breathing heavily.

A delightful panorama spread before their gaze. In the distance, the sun shone upon the city's lake and temples. Groves of oak, camphor and gingko trees covered the land.

Clarence took a deep breath. 'How peaceful it is here.' His thoughts flew to his family back home. *Had the Nazis left them in peace to get on with life?*

'I'll never forget the dive bombers sounding like hornets, the anti-aircraft guns and machine-gun fire,' he said, casting his mind back to the London raids.

Parry nodded. 'Remember the time they got the ARP post and we tried to dig the bombs out?'

'You thought you felt a sewer pipe in the dark, but it turned out to be a time-bomb. We had to evacuate the survivors who had been in the recreation room. Lucky for them the bomb didn't explode or they'd have all gone to Old Glory.'

Parry combed his hair back with his fingers. 'Wonder how Angus and Albert are.'

Clarence recalled their time together in London during the Blitz and thought of the eighteen months he'd been in Calcutta with them. 'They're probably busy. The heat and humidity gets one down in India. We can't grumble about that here. The weather in Yunnan is ideal. But stay healthy. Hospital facilities are not too good in China.' He slapped him on the back. 'Just try not to get dysentery, cholera, typhus, malaria or plague, chum.'

His words sent the muscles twitching across Parry's face. Clarence noticed a shadow of despondency falling upon him, and tried to break through the crust of reserve his friend now wore like a breast-plate. A forest of thoughts sprouted. *Please God, tell me how to help him*, Clarence prayed, and, realising that speaking would release his feelings, he decided to stop trying to ignore his friend's unhappiness.

'Let's make the most of today,' he said in as jovial a voice as he could muster.

Parry only compressed his lips and stared straight ahead.

Clarence puckered his brows. 'How's life been treating you?'

'I work on the Kutsing-Luhsien run. Carry medical supplies to Luhsein. Return with commercial cargo to Kutsing.' He clamped his teeth together and the muscles in his jaws were working.

'I believe it's tough on that route.'

'Road turns torturous and slippery during rainy weather.' Then Parry's words cascaded out, the Welsh lilt edging back into his voice. 'Difficult to prevent the truck from skidding over the cliffs. At Luhsein, skin turned yellow. Couldn't eat. Diagnosis—jaundice. Remained in bed for ten days until fit enough to travel.'

Clarence shook his head and whistled. 'I'm sorry. I didn't hear about your illness.'

'Bad for morale.'

'Fully recovered now?'

'Still recuperating. Sent down to Kunming for a change. You're the best tonic for body and soul.' Parry smiled, but his eyes remained dull.

'How's your friend, Grace?'

'Her father used his influence as an ex-public service official. Had her transferred to Calcutta.' Parry sighed. 'She's married now.'

'That must be a terrible blow for you.'

'Absolutely heartbroken. My pride is wounded too.'

Clarence remembered what he felt like when he and Mary had quarrelled, and prayed for his friend, although this was something that often happened to Parry.

Two months' later, Parry confided, 'I've been bitten by the love bug.'

Clarence laughed. 'Who's it this time?'

'Met Barbara Hamilton? Works for the International Red Cross at Kunming. She's from Denver. Says I'll be welcome anytime I'm over there.'

'It doesn't look like the war will ever end,' Clarence said. 'By then you'll have forgotten her.'

'I'll never forget Barbara,' Parry answered. 'Her soft brown hair and warm, friendly eyes are absolutely alluring.'

Clarence's thoughts turned to Mary—their meetings at Fellowship gatherings and the warmth of her smile. *O God, how I love her. Please keep her safe, and if it is Your will, let her wait for me.*

In August 1944, Clarence received his first letter from Doug since his arrival in Yunnan.

By October, the blackout in England was over as Germany, like a cornered animal, was now on the defensive and in no position to bomb the country. Roy was stationed at Chilwell, which was near enough to where Stan and Anne lived. He visited them most evenings.

The following month Doug wrote two more letters in the same strain. Then a month went by with no word from him.

Clarence gnawed at his nails in a frenzy of suspense.

CHAPTER 19

VISIT TO CHUNGKING

Chungking, January 1945

The threat to Chungking subsided when two divisions of General Stilwell's well-trained X Force arrived to defend the airfield at Kunming. Not long after, John Rossi offered Clarence a flight to Chungking in return for helping load the plane with supplies.

'We'll have a look at the place before we fly back,' he promised.

Clarence left a message for Bill and followed John with long, rapid strides. After a tricky three hour flight, he had his first glimpse of Chungking's aerodrome—a small patch of baked earth surrounded by mountains.

'You're lucky,' John said on landing. 'The whole field is usually covered by cloud and shrouded in a veil of mist.'

After unloading their cargo, he borrowed a jeep and drove Clarence to the city. On their way in, they visited John's missionary friends, Harry and Elizabeth Gould. Clarence longed to remain longer and talk about their lives as missionaries, but time was limited, and they were forced to leave.

At the edge of the metropolis, they passed the Chinese military camp.

'The militia is safe here from the nightly air raids on Chungking,' John said. 'The enemy's aim is not so much as to destroy the army, but to terrorise the civilian population and cause chaos.'

They've succeeded in terrorising them, Clarence thought, *but they've also strengthened their resolve to die fighting the enemy.*

Chungking was situated on the mountains overlooking the Yangtse. Hovels in the clefs of cliffs housed the poor, and filth from open drains on either side of the road found its way into the river. Clarence gazed at coolies staggering up stone steps with buckets of water for wealthy residents on the hill. Others lurched downhill, carrying loads of human refuse for use as manure in the fields below. Even from a distance, the disgusting odour drifted down to them whenever the wind blew in their direction.

'The water is so polluted that every drop has to be boiled before one can drink it,' John explained. He parked the vehicle and paid a couple of urchins to watch his jeep while he and Clarence left to investigate the results of Japanese raids.

Japanese bombers had spared nothing. Only a few houses had escaped the bombing. The smell of cordite and smoke still hung around the streets, and snarled coils of electric wire clung from wrecked homes.

Clarence rubbed his nose with his forefinger. 'Where are the air raid shelters?'

'They're at the foot of the hills. The tunnels are about seven feet wide, with only standing room in the dark interior. They use the entrance as a toilet, so the place stinks and is full of flies.'

Clarence recalled the London Blitz and compared their air raid shelters to the ones at Chungking. He shivered. How much worse off the people over here were.

'The Chinese have stood fast, despite the fire and destruction,' John said. 'Thousands work in underground factories and continue working during raids.'

Clarence nodded. He couldn't trust himself to say anything lest his voice trembled and he betrayed the feelings that wrenched his heart—pity for them and anger against the Japanese.

Vendors, their little stalls lit by tiny flaming torches that exaggerated the red of the tomatoes and oranges, lined the broad, paved streets. People were shouting and gesticulating.

'What's going on?' Clarence asked.

'They're only bargaining,' John said with a laugh. Then he slapped his hip pocket and turned to Clarence. 'I forgot to warn you about pickpockets.'

Clarence instinctively felt for his wallet. *Still there in spite of all the pushing and jostling.* A pair of fur slippers caught his eye. They would keep his feet warm on cold winter evenings.

Clarence had learned the art of bargaining in India but he refined his methods in China.

'Always remember the rules of Chinese courtesy,' Bill had told him, during his first weeks at Kunming. 'The important thing is to never appear in a hurry to clinch a bargain.'

People gathered around, spitting and hawking, listening to him as he haggled over the price, bringing it down as far as he could.

After his purchase, the two men hurried back to the jeep.

John pressed his foot on the accelerator. 'We must be off before the raid starts tonight, unless we wish to sleep in one of the shelters.'

At that time, Parry was based at Chungking, and Clarence hoped to visit him before they returned to Kunming. Reluctant to take advantage of John, and debating whether to impose on their friendship, he waited for the opportune moment to broach the subject. A few hours of daylight still remained. He had not seen Parry for months and his desire to meet him again was so strong that he no longer could refrain from asking for another favour.

'Will we have time to pop in and say hello to my friend, Parry Davies?' Clarence asked.

'Of course we can,' John answered. 'Why didn't you ask me earlier?'

He sped to the FAU quarters and on their arrival, the Chinese houseboy led them upstairs.

Clarence slipped the boy a coin and entered Parry's room. They found him lying on his back, his arms thrown above his head. He lay fully clothed, as if he'd just flung himself on the bed and fallen asleep.

Parry worked on the Chungking-Kweiyang run during those perilous times. The route was appalling. Rough roads rattled trucks, like a cat shaking the life out of a rat, and sharp rocks tore tyres to shreds. Mechanics had to rebuild the vehicles after each trip.

Clarence glanced down at the prone figure of his friend. 'He's probably catching up with sleep after taking supplies to remote areas.'

The crunch of their boots on the bare floor must have awakened Parry. His eyes fluttered open. He half rose and swore in Chinese but dropped back on his pillow.

Clarence peered down at him, turning pale to find his friend so worn out. 'How are you, chum? You look like death warmed up. Sorry to disturb you.'

Parry raised himself on his elbow. 'Pretty tough dodging bombs. My driver, Roy Sun, developed carbuncles on his arse. Agonising on rough roads. No medic along. Sterilised cutthroat-razor in boiling water. Lanced boils. Slept in a cave last night but drove off this morning.'

He paused and raised his eyebrows. 'How come you're here?'

'John gave me a lift in his plane. I've never been to Chungking and wanted to come in case the Japs get in and I don't have another chance to see the city.'

'You're not cheerful today,' Parry said, falling back on his pillow.

John laid his hand on Parry's shoulder. 'Just go to sleep, buddy.'

Clarence shook hands. 'Goodbye.'

'See you soon, man.' Parry closed his eyes.

'He'll fall asleep even before the sound of our boots on the stairs fade,' Clarence said.

They hurried back to the jeep. The city seemed to hold its breath as they sped to the airport and took off before the thunder of enemy planes rocked it.

Back at Kunming, ground crewmen guided John, who swung the plane ninety degrees, and parked alongside other craft. The ticking sound of hot metal echoed from beneath its wings as the hatch swung open, and Clarence dropped on the tarmac with a thud.

No sooner had Clarence and John stepped on firm ground than an open truck pulled up for them. Before leaving for his quarters, Clarence thanked the airman for the trip to Chungking, not knowing if he'd ever see him again.

CHAPTER 20

THE KUNMING – HANOI RAIL JOURNEY

Kunming, April 1945

One day, Bill visited Clarence while he was busy packing stores in the Nissan hut. 'Your gaunt figure scarcely casts a shadow upon the ground. Time you had a break. Would you like to have a trip to Hanoi? Our Chinese cook will accompany you.'

Clarence's strained features scrunched into a grin. 'Marvellous. I believe you can buy anything there.'

Bill nodded. 'Ah Fong will be going there to get some supplies tomorrow. Get ready to join him. Drop in at my office on your way back after work and I'll give you your travel expenses.'

Trains linked Japanese-occupied territory and areas still under the Kuomintang regime, where trade in goods carried on. Yunnan was rich in vegetables, cereals and fruits, so cooks and mess sergeants sold food supplies to the enemy and purchased items from stores at Hanoi.

The constant rain had obliterated the paint on the second-class carriage they boarded. Clarence chose a window seat facing the front, though it was wooden and uncomfortable.

Ah Fong dragged his basket of fruit and vegetables to the passage but kept it within sight in case of theft, and took the seat opposite Clarence. His black hair shone in the sun and his tawny skin glowed. He sat cross-legged on a red satin cushion and glanced at his goods every now and then. Every so often he would uncross his short, podgy legs, massage them with his fingers and pummel them with his fists.

Clarence placed his hands on his knees and moved his head from side to side, surveying the passing scenery. Steep pine-covered hills flashed past and streams snaked through the jungle. Colourful orchids festooned the trees and azaleas covered the forest floor—a sharp contrast to his rail trip across the great Indian continent.

The journey to Hanoi took five days. Ah Fong had brought along a roll of two-inch broad bamboo planks tied together with cane, and at nights, he laid them across the opposite seats to form a bed for them to curl up and sleep.

The engine only paused long enough for passengers to embark or disembark and buy food before steaming off again, ascending hills and passing through tunnels. Clarence leaned back in his seat, hummed to himself and let the warmth spread throughout his body as he rocked to the rhythm of the wheels on the rails.

When the train arrived at Hanoi, travellers leapt to their feet, gathered up their luggage and shuffled along the narrow aisles. The weather at Kunming had been a pleasant twenty to twenty-four degrees, but the heat and dust here reminded Clarence of Calcutta. Ah Fong pointed out the shops selling Western goods and hailed a passing rickshaw. He placed his basket of fruit and vegetables in with him and headed for the market to sell them. He had arranged for accommodation with a friend.

Feeling the need for exercise after the long train trip, Clarence sauntered down to the up-market area. Luxuries of all kinds filled the stores. A bottle of French perfume caught his attention, and his heart took flight to Mary. *What was she wearing now? What fragrance?* He could barely afford the money, but he bought a small vial and knew her thoughts would turn to him each time she wore his gift.

Clarence knew Eva would love a leather handbag. He haggled over the price and brought it down as low as he could, before paying the vendor.

He booked a room at a hotel for three nights and spent the days sightseeing and shopping.

Before their return trip, Ah Fong engaged a coolie to wheel two baskets of tinned provisions into a third-class compartment, where he had booked a seat. Clarence used his return ticket to travel in a second-class carriage. He watched the train threading across the night like a luminous caterpillar. They passed through eight tunnels without any mishap but at the ninth tunnel, the engine commenced slipping. Unable to take the strain, a coupling snapped. The locomotive continued down the track, while the carriages slid back downhill, gaining momentum as they went faster and faster. Pandemonium broke out. Men swore, children cried, and women clung to their babies or their seats.

Clarence, who had been sitting wrapped up in his blanket, rose in alarm. He shivered as the cold wind blew and drove him back to his warm seat. He pulled up his blanket and settled down again.

After careering down at an alarming rate, the train stopped in the middle of a long tunnel. A passenger shone a torch and stepped outside to investigate. After a few minutes, he returned and clambered into his seat before switching off his flashlight.

Half an hour or so later, the engine steamed back and stopped at the base near the carriages. It was obvious that a coupling had snapped just as they had reached the crest of the hill and the engine driver had steamed ahead, oblivious of what had happened.

A voice stabbed the darkness. 'The driver is probably looking for the lost train.'

With a broken link, they wouldn't be able to connect to the locomotive, and no one knew how long the repair would take. Passengers made themselves as comfortable as they could and settled back to sleep for the rest of the night. At dawn, light filtered through chinks in the slats of the wooden window. Clarence threw off his blanket, folded it, and went out in the fresh air. By then, the engine crew were squatting in a circle, shouting and gesticulating.

An hour passed before one of the men got up and headed towards a partly-hidden valley.

Shortly after, he returned with three feet of wire. The workers used the material as a coupling and attached the carriages to the locomotive, pounding the metal into place with a rock. Clarence hurried back to the train, knowing they soon would be leaving.

A weasel-eyed man about five feet two inches in height with an olive complexion now sat in his seat. His eyebrows hung over his eyes like a boxer. His nose was flattish, probably from the number of hits it had taken, and his clothes were crumpled as if he had picked them off the floor and flung them on in a hurry.

Clarence had left his blanket on his seat to indicate it was occupied, but the intruder had pushed it to one side. He flushed and his voice rose. 'Excuse me. This is my place.'

'Pardon, *monsieur*,' the stranger replied. 'There is sufficient room for us both, no?' He moved over for Clarence, who didn't want to cause a scene.

Clarence squeezed back into his seat. The stale odour of tobacco stifled him. He wondered who this Frenchie was.

The man smoothed his jacket and rubbed his nicotine-stained fingers together. *It could only mean nervousness or stress. Perhaps he longed for a cigarette.* He fumbled in his pocket.

If he gets out a packet of cigarettes and attempts to smoke, it'll be the last straw, Clarence thought, but the man held out a bar of chocolate to Clarence.

'No thanks.' Clarence fisted his hands to ward off the temptation of accepting anything from a total stranger.

'I have another. Please accept this.'

Unable to resist the offer a second time, Clarence reached out and looked at the peace offering. 'Thank you.'

The man's sallow face broke into a smile. Clarence tore off the wrapper and took a bite. He shut his eyes and rolled the piece of chocolate over his tongue, enjoying the flavour. *How did Froggie get hold of this delicious treat?* If it was meant to placate him, it certainly did that.

The Frenchman tilted his head towards Clarence and appeared to be studying him, but he said nothing until the train moved off. 'My name is Pierre.'

'Clarence. How do you do?'

'I journey to Kunming to join the FAU.' He glanced at the epaulets on Clarence's uniform, which bore the letters FAU. 'You are a member. You can help me. Yes?'

'I'll put in a word for you to the boss. What was your occupation before the war?'

'I was in the Foreign Legion. I escaped from the Japanese and journeyed far through tortuous jungle.'

'Then why join a non-fighting unit like mine?'

'Sick and starving, I found *mon Dieu*. War is evil. I desire peace.'

Clarence's heart warmed towards the stranger. *So that's why he was gazing at me.*

'I'll speak to my superior officers and perhaps make an appointment for you. How may I contact you?'

'If you give me details of your residence, I'll come and see you,' Pierre said.

Clarence took out his notebook, wrote down his address at Kunming, tore off the page and handed it to Pierre. *The unit could do with an extra hand.* Too many members were either sick or exhausted, and he knew that Bill had given him time off to visit Hanoi only because of the old adage that all work and no play made Jack a dull boy.

Soon after his return, Clarence told Bill about the Frenchman, but Bill was doubtful of engaging someone whose background they knew nothing of. 'He may be a Vichy French spy for all we know,' he said.

Clarence recalled Bill's warning to him about the Vichy French when he'd first arrived. He swept the thought aside. The man had repented of his wild ways. 'If he's changed his ways, surely we should give him a chance? Besides, it would ease the burden on the rest of us.'

'I'd rather not take the risk,' Bill said, pounding his fist on the table.

Clarence's brows shot up. *Everyone seems to be on a short fuse these days!*

When Pierre came over to see him, Clarence expressed his regret at not being able to arrange an interview for him.

The Frenchman pursed his lips so hard that for a moment they disappeared. Then he shrugged. 'But we can still be comrades, no? Do you like French cuisine? Let me take you to an excellent restaurant.'

'I cannot impose upon you,' Clarence replied.

'*Mon Dieu. Pas de probleme.* I am in luck. Look.'

He took out a wallet filled with notes. 'A comrade left me this before he died. Now you will accept? When can you come?'

Clarence could not refuse such an offer. It sounded tempting. Even at home, he seldom had the luxury of indulging in French food. He arranged to meet Pierre in the evening.

The cafe had red tablecloths and napkins with baguette slices and butter at every table. Fifty seats filled the interior, with another fifty outside in a garden setting. Waiters wove around tables, balancing trays of food and drinks. One came up to them, and Pierre requested a table for two near a corner.

The aroma of cooking drifted from the kitchen. Overhead, shelves held bottles of liqueur neatly stacked in pyramids. The array of cakes behind the glass counter brought to mind the rare luxury of high tea when on holiday in Scotland before the war.

Clarence ordered an entrée of steamed mussels and cream in wine sauce served with French fries. The main course included a Caesar salad and smoked salmon, garnished with field greens, capers and shallots.

The crunchy salad and delicious salmon soon disappeared, and Clarence waited, his salivary glands active, during the long delay for dessert. He had a slice of rich chocolate cake sprinkled with caramel and almonds. The cake slipped down once it arrived, and nothing but crumbs remained on the plate. The dinner was delightful. A change from Ah Fong's meals.

Pierre seemed a good sort, and the conversation turned to the work Clarence was currently doing.

'I'm in charge of supplies and also help load and unload planes whenever the airport is busy.'

Pierre nodded. 'I would be glad to be of service anytime.'

When they were about to leave, Clarence tugged his ear. 'Sorry, we couldn't find you a job. Perhaps something will turn up later.'

'I'll come and visit you, if you can spare the time,' Pierre said.

'Yes. Drop in anytime and I'll treat you to some American food at their cafeteria.' The USAAF canteen welcomed members of the FAU, and Clarence relaxed over a coke or conversed with the others in between unloading, unpacking and distributing stores.

'*Oui*, that is good. I will be your guest. Next week is just before Christmas. Is that too soon?'

'No. Do come. We'll meet on Monday then.'

'*Bon, bon. Au revoir.*'

On Monday, when Pierre joined Clarence for the promised meal, the canteen was crowded. Orderlies were putting up Christmas decorations and pilots continually dropped in for a strong cup of coffee to keep them awake. Someone was singing, *White Christmas*.

When the song ended, a sergeant called out, 'Hi Clarence, Father Christmas will be leaving for Chungking within the next hour. Hurry up.'

'What's up?' Clarence asked.

'We need help to load the plane,' he said, moving off.

Pierre picked up his serviette and wiped his lips. 'I will not keep you any longer, comrade. Thank you for the repast. Merry Christmas.'

Clarence strode towards the counter and paid the bill. He hurried along to his quarters, knowing the men needed a hand to load their Christmas fare.

The unusually heavy meal he had eaten brought on a cramp in his stomach, compelling him to slow down, and by the time he arrived at his room, the sun had set and the temperature had dropped several degrees. He changed his clothes and pulled on a thick jumper.

While ascending the stairs, he heard the roar of planes. Enemy fighters flew in first and strafed the airfield, then bombers followed. They scored a direct hit on the supply plane just loaded with mail and Christmas dinner for the troops at Chungking. The earth heaved, spitting dirt. Steel fragments flew in all directions. The aircraft caught fire and was incinerated, killing a ground crew airman.

Clarence sprinted down the stairs, and his boots pounded the tarmac as he flew towards the scene of disaster. Charred pieces of paper and the smell of burned turkey hung over the place. Clarence helped clear the wreckage. The stench of scorched flesh seeped into his clothes and the heat from the tarmac filtered through his boots, making his face crimson.

Chinese coolies filled the bomb craters with gravel, and the next plane brought in fresh supplies of festive fare, but the men had to do without their mail. The boys at Chungking would gladly have forfeited the turkey for letters from home. This was war, however, so no one grumbled.

For nights after the bombing, Clarence tossed and turned in bed. With a wrinkled brow, he evaluated Pierre's behaviour and mentally ran through his actions and words. *Did the Frenchman have something to do with the disaster? Was it just coincidental that the planes came in soon after he'd left?* Clarence couldn't shake the feeling that he was to blame for the calamity. He tried to convince himself that he couldn't have known whether Pierre was a spy. If he spoke to Bill about it, his boss would only pass on the information to the Americans who were likely to send out search parties and raze the countryside. If they found nothing, he'd have wasted their precious time.

Clarence had no one to turn to for advice. His close friend Parry was miles away. He had only one alternative—to prove the Frenchman's innocence or guilt. He'd search for his hideout, if he had one.

Clarence climbed the hill near the warehouse from which he often watched the dogfights above. He scanned the hills surrounding the airstrip. They were dotted by rocks, bushes and almond trees. *Perhaps Pierre had a radio tucked in somewhere?*

That evening, after the houseboy had finished his chores, Clarence told him to accompany him. He carried a small flashlight, a penknife and a piece of string in his pocket. He grabbed a stick to serve as a cudgel, if necessary, and set out on his quest—a habit left over from his childhood days when the four brothers played cops and robbers.

No path covered the slopes. Clarence battled uphill, intent on allaying his suspicions once and for all. They traced their way among swamps and hills, ascending ravines and plunging into bogs intersected by streams. Trees and thickets ran up the sides of the hill and disappeared amidst the chasms.

After an uphill slog for fifteen minutes, the hillside grew more rugged. The houseboy carried a long carving knife. Now he used it as a scythe, cutting a path for them. 'What you looking for?' he asked, in Pidgin English.

'A cave.'

'You want bat shit for garden?'

'No.' Clarence shook his head. He had no idea what he was searching for. *A hide-out? A radio?* He forced his way past rocks and thorny bushes that scratched his limbs. His fingers grew numb with the cold. Thickly tangled growth barred their path.

The boy stopped slashing the undergrowth and stared upwards. The creepers reached far above his head, but no tree held them up. Clarence skirted the vines, searching for an opening, or disturbed vegetation. Creepers needed something for support. Yet these appeared to stand by themselves.

To his surprise, he caught a faint odour of tobacco as the wind blew towards him and, looking carefully, he discovered an opening covered by a few vines.

'A cave!' He flashed his torch and illuminated the dark interior. On the ground were a few cigarette butts that had been crushed underfoot. He imagined the Frenchman chain smoking while waiting for something. If he is a spy, where was the radio he used to transmit the message? Clarence searched behind every stone and crevice but discovered nothing.

Who had been smoking in the cave and what was he doing? 'Let's look outside,' he said.

The houseboy slashed the surrounding bushes and vines. Still no evidence turned up. The sun was now low in the sky and it would soon be dark. They scrambled down the hill, keeping to the side opposite the airstrip. A footpath clung to the slope for a while, before slithering down to a swamp. The smell of rotting vegetation assaulted their noses and a high-pitched whining filled the air.

A black cloud of mosquitoes assailed them, attacking every exposed square inch of their bodies. Clarence slapped them away from his face and arms, while the boy fled. He followed—a cloud of mosquitoes behind him.

The lad was yards ahead, but still within hearing. Clarence heard him struggling among the dense undergrowth. Scrambling down across rocks and through bushes, he tripped and bruised his elbows, but he had escaped from the fury of the mosquitoes. He got up and hastened his steps, taking care to watch where he went, heading in the same direction as the houseboy, making his way along the high ground, away from the marsh and up again.

He heard a cry ahead, and ran forward. His companion had fallen, face down. A thorny cane entangled his clothes. Within minutes, Clarence gently removed the vine from the sobbing boy and hauled him to his feet. The sight of his bruised and swollen visage was dreadful.

He guessed his own mosquito-bitten face and limbs were no different. He rubbed his arms to relieve the itching, taking care not to use his nails and cause infection.

They followed the contours of the thickly-wooded hill down, through a gully. Skirting the knoll, they came in sight of the airstrip in the distance. The trees finally started to thin out.

Exhausted, they flopped down and paused for breath. Clarence hoped he wouldn't run into Bill on the way back and have to explain his scratches and bites. He felt foolish and didn't want to lose face before his houseboy.

He'd remained out longer than he had intended and knew the boy would merit a cuff on his ear from the kitchen hand. Delving into his pocket, he took out a coin. 'Nice work,' he said, handing it to the youngster.

The boy ducked his head several times. 'Thank you. Thank you.'

Clarence guessed the lad had been amply rewarded for his pain, but the itching annoyed him. Nothing had come of his day's adventure. Neither had it left him with peace of mind. Perhaps he should have listened to the more experienced man. After all, Bill had mentioned his doubts of Pierre from the start.

Still he hesitated.

He longed for a hot bath and a cup of tea. Perhaps it would ease the itching and help him think clearly.

After a shower, Clarence gazed out of the window, took a sip of tea and shook his head. He repeated the words, *help me, Lord* several times, lips glittering with Earl Grey as they moved.

All the uncomfortable moments of the day nudged him into worrying whether he could have done better. Had he been able to read into the future, he'd have taken action earlier.

CHAPTER 21

WAR AND PEACE

Kunming, June 1945

A few days after his misadventure in the surrounding hills, Clarence awoke, lethargic and irritable. That evening, overtaken by nausea, he rushed to the lavatory. His head ached and a burning thirst consumed him.

Bill met him as he staggered back from the toilet. 'Are you alright? You look flushed and your eyes are red.'

'I've a raging headache and a temperature.'

Bill took his pulse. 'Go to bed. I'll send for a doctor.'

Old Doc Dwyer came as soon as possible. By the time he arrived, Clarence lay shivering beneath a pile of blankets. His teeth chattered and his temperature had risen even higher. The light from the windows hurt his eyes and sounds from the kitchen aggravated him.

Doc Dwyer took his temperature. 'You have malaria. Rest is the only cure. Remain in bed until I say you may get up. Meanwhile, take these tablets and drink lots of water. You won't want food, but get as much sleep as possible.'

Clarence hardly remembered the days he spent in bed. Confined to his room, unaware of his surroundings, he curled up into a ball like a sick dog, only wanting to be alone—neither caring for anyone nor anything. The glass of water by his bedside remained untouched until someone put it to his lips. At times, gentle hands wiped the perspiration from his brow and helped him sit up, before removing his drenched clothes.

Weeks later, weak and hungry, Clarence raised his head from the pillow. 'Any food around?'

Doc Dywer, who had just walked into the room, placed his hands on his hips and laughed. The sunspots on the bald patch in the middle of his head seemed to glow, and the two wings of white hair on either side shone like a halo. 'That's a good sign. The danger has passed. You may take a shower. I'll tell cook to bring you a bowl of hot, nourishing chicken soup.'

Bill hurried in soon after. 'Glad you're feeling better. Your French friend was hanging around the canteen. Said he was looking for you. Somehow, I don't trust him. The raids have increased since he's been here, and the enemy seem to know when our planes come in with a load of supplies.' He paused. 'Makes you wonder, doesn't it?'

Bill had asked a rhetorical question, but Clarence went rigid and felt his face suffused with blood. He breathed two or three times before he managed to get himself under control. *What was Bill saying? Was he trying to insinuate that Pierre was not to be trusted? Or worse still, that he was a spy?* Clarence wrinkled his brow and bit his lip, thinking about Pierre. *Was he a spy?* He thought of the possible repercussions if he revealed his doubts to Bill. *If only Parry were here. He could talk to him without starting a witch-hunt. What should he do?*

Weak in mind and body after his brush with death, the thought of having befriended a spy tormented him. He needed to hang on to the back of a chair or the edge of a table for support when walking.

He was not yet ready to confront Pierre.

It took another month before Clarence's health returned to normal. He knew he was fortunate he'd not fallen ill while on the road. What would he have done then? Perhaps his Chinese mechanic would have had to take over and drive him to the nearest destination. All too often, when members of the FAU could not be treated in China, planes flew serious and recurrent cases across the Hump to hospitals in Calcutta. His duty was here. He didn't want to return to India.

Clarence met Parry during his next trip to Kutsing and went straight to the point. I've wanted to discuss something with you for a long time. Do you remember the Frenchman, Pierre, who I encountered on the train?'

'You did mention him. Why?'

'Well. Seems that whenever he's seen around, we lose a plane or two. Bill thinks that enemy raids occur not long after ours land—while they are being unloaded—and Pierre's never there *during* the bombing.'

'Too coincidental, don't you think?' Parry asked.

'Yes. But what can I do? Should I report him or tell him not to come here any longer?' He clenched his fists. He had learned to keep the knot of his anger tied up. Now it burst its bounds. 'I could shoot him myself if he turns out to be a spy.'

His sudden outburst amazed him. He reigned his fury in. 'So many Free French are in Kunming. Surely they'd know if he's not one of them.'

Parry slid his fingers through his hair. 'He uses the French Indochina–Yunnan railway quite often. Indochina is governed by the pro-Nazi Vichy French …'

Clarence turned pale. 'Perhaps he gets his orders from Hanoi and spies for the Japs.'

Parry hit his left palm with his fist and swore. 'I say he should be stopped.'

'What can I do? I can't betray a friend if he's innocent, but if he has been using me, it's intolerable. I'd like to throttle him with my bare hands.' His voice rose and his eyebrows soared as he spoke.

'If bombers turn up soon after his departure, you should scour the countryside. He must have a wireless hidden nearby.'

'I've done that and haven't unearthed a clue.'

'Just can't sit back and do nothing, man. Perhaps you should report it to Bill.'

Consumed by guilt, Clarence discussed the matter with Bill the next day.

Bill placed his hand on Clarence's shoulder. 'Cheer up. Look on the bright side. You need some fun. We've been invited to dine with one of the Chinese generals. An invitation to a meal promotes a sense of *bonhomie*.'

His kind and understanding manner soon put Clarence at rest.

Bill reported his suspicions to General Chennault and a detail of US servicemen scoured the cave. Finding a crack in the floor, they cleared the dirt from around and prised it open. It turned out to be a slab of concrete concealing a space containing a transmitter.

Pierre never turned up at the canteen again. Japanese air raids continued randomly, but they no longer flew in each time supply planes landed.

Not long after the liberation of France in the summer of 1944, Japanese imprisoned most Frenchmen, but Pierre remained free.

When the news reached Kunming, all doubts of his duplicity vanished. Clarence mentally berated himself over his procrastination and apologised to Bill, who simply said, 'We all make mistakes, brother,' and patted him on his shoulder.

Clarence never saw the French spy again, but once the Allies regained control of Hanoi, rumours spread that he'd met with summary justice. A sense of gratification came over Clarence.

Before leaving for the dinner with the Chinese generals, Bill forewarned, 'They eat noisily, as they believe that food should be aerated to relish its flavour.'

At the banquet, servants handed out hot moist towels for guests to wipe their hands and face. Fish, garnished with ginger and sauce, and dozens of other rich and varied dishes graced the table. Scores of little blue and white porcelain bowls contained dainties like larks' tongues and hundred-year-old eggs.

The host praised Britain and the United States. Guests reciprocated in praise of Chaing Kai-Shek and nationalist China. Between courses, each guest sipped a small glass of rice wine. Custom dictated that they drain the last drop. Clarence pretended to drink, and succeeded in disposing of his wine unobtrusively by pouring it into an empty soup bowl.

Bill had taught Clarence how to use chopsticks, but he could barely satisfy his hunger with them. He longed for a knife and fork. The Chinese clutched their food bowls, using their twin sticks to send a stream of rice and lumps of meat into their mouths.

Clarence listened to the conversation, but in spite of all his study of the Chinese language, he failed to understand a word. He soon gave up trying to pick out something familiar.

He also found it difficult to put the right accent on words.

'The pitch and rhythm of one's voice is important,' Bill had told him. 'Be careful, especially at dinner, as the word *pig* could stand for *lord* with the incorrect pitch.'

Clarence knew it was good for people of different cultures to get to know each other, despite their ignorance of each other's tongues, and believed that mixing with the locals was an efficient way of acquiring a language. He socialised with the Chinese staff and they helped him in his pronunciation, entertaining him with fascinating stories of their country at the same time.

One stifling hot day, he and Peter Tong, a Chinese Christian who had been studying at the Chengtu University at the outbreak of war, stopped at a wayside stall and ordered a pot of tea together. The acid smoke of charcoal fires rose from tin smelters beyond Kunming's thirty-foot high city walls. On the cobblestone street, herdsmen in blue jackets and baggy trousers drove their goats to market. A line of children came from the factory, dragging their feet and stumbling along with slumped shoulders, their throats swollen, their skin green from arsenic poisoning.

Clarence's eyes narrowed. He longed to be able to alleviate their pain, but there was nothing he could do for them. He turned to his companion.

Peter must have read the sympathy in his eyes. 'The children have no choice. They need the money for sustenance. We all cling to life,' he said.

The waiter brought out a pot of tea and poured the steaming brew into their cups. The aroma rose to greet Clarence as he waited for his tea to cool. He wiped the sweat from his brow. 'What would we do without our cup of tea?'

Peter smiled, exposing a row of yellowing teeth. 'You and Bill must visit our humble home one day and partake of my mother's tea.'

'I'd love to. There are so many varieties. I never know which to choose.'

Peter slurped his tea. 'We grow a thousand different kinds in China, but in general, there are five types.'

'I've heard that tea has many medicinal uses,' Clarence said, eager to learn more about his favourite brew.

'Yes. Yes. It is cooling and relaxing and helps digestion. We say, "Better to go without salt for three days than drink no tea for one day." Tea, like chop-sticks, is part of our culture.' Peter made a broad sweep with his hand.

Relaxed and refreshed, Clarence smiled, enjoying the peace and quiet he loved so well.

A few weeks later, Clarence and Bill visited Peter's house, a simple dwelling with an earthen floor. Peter's mother served tea at a low wooden table. She lined up the blue and white porcelain bowls close together in a row, holding the matching teapot aloft. With her arm moving slowly over them, she filled the four cups in one sweep. All the while, its fragrance drifted upwards to the guests, creating a tranquil atmosphere.

Clarence sat on a small stool and watched, fascinated by the graceful manner with which she poured the tea. Peter was right. His mother's tea had something special about it. Somehow, the tea was unlike the one they'd had at the teashop. Nor was it like Ah Fong's brew. It left a velvety feeling on his tongue and brought on a kind of euphoria.

Back at their quarters, the smell of mushrooms and duck wafted from the kitchen. Clarence grew hungry. To divert attention from his stomach, which was beginning to growl, he made small talk, 'John Cadbury sold tea in his shop in Birmingham.'

Bill nodded. 'Both Harrods and Lloyds had humble beginnings and traded in tea during the mid-nineteenth century.'

Clarence enjoyed piecing together the past. 'Years back, a botanist planted tea on the foot-hills of the Himalayas in Assam. That's how we got Darjeeling tea.'

'Now it's part of our culture and so many songs have been written of our favourite brew. The plays, *Tea and Sympathy* and *Teahouse of the August Moon*—not to mention the famous song …'

They both burst out singing a few lines of the popular piece,
Just tea for two and two for tea,
Just me for you and you for me alone …'

Ah Fong came running out from the kitchen, perspiration streaming down his face. 'Chaing-Kai-shek won victory?'

'No. Nothing like that. We need to cheer ourselves.'

The cook beamed. 'Understand, sir.'

'He was anxious to know what had caused this sudden outburst,' Bill explained to Clarence.

They yawned, turned the lights out and went into the dining room without waiting for the dinner gong.

The days were growing colder and shorter. Japanese aircraft dropped typhus and cholera cultures on wells and ponds in Yunnan, and two members of the FAU succumbed to typhus from the epidemic that followed. Everyone flinched at the thought of contracting the disease.

In December, an American medic visited Clarence in the warehouse at Kunming. He handed several rattraps to him. 'Winter is a bad time for plague. You've all been inoculated, but no one is immune. I suggest you set these regularly. Can't trust your Chinese cook. He may take the rat home to feed his cats. They breed cats for eating, you know.'

Clarence searched his face, thinking he had been joking about ingesting the furry felines but the doctor remained unsmiling. 'Make sure you kill the varmints. Japanese planes have dropped plague-infected fleas in China and now we have an epidemic.'

With such a stringent warning from the doctor, Clarence wasted no time in setting traps before retiring for the night.

Early the next morning he inspected the snares. Enormous rats bared their fangs at him from five of the six traps. He stared at the entrapped vermin. How could he kill them without opening the cages?

Carefully, with hammer in hand, he eased open one of the traps a tiny fraction, hoping to hit the rodent when its head stuck out. The rat let out a hiss and scampered off before Clarence could hit it. He followed, landing a heavy blow on it, but the cornered rat turned, spitting and snarling.

Clarence stepped back, surprised.

The rodent raced towards him and sought refuge in his trousers. It clambered up his right leg, scratching his thigh with its sharp claws, and snuggled down below his belt.

Clarence dropped the hammer, letting out a roar that carried through to the rest of the building. Then he stood still, afraid it would commence gnawing his vital parts.

Fortunately, the doctor, who was expecting a planeload of wounded from the frontline, had stopped for the night at Kunming. When he heard the shout, he rushed into the warehouse. 'Unfasten your belt and let down your trousers,' he shouted as soon as he saw what had occurred.

In his hurry to follow instructions, Clarence's hands were clumsy, but he finally succeeded in removing his belt. When his slacks slid to the ground, the rat ran, snarling and snapping, to safety. What deadly disease had he caught from the vermin? In a daze, he gazed at the scratches on his leg.

The doctor laughed. 'You're lucky it only just ran up your leg. You never know what you may catch. Wash the cuts with an antiseptic. In the future, pour boiling water on it. That'll kill it soon enough. Fortunately, the plague season hasn't started.'

Clarence shuddered to think of his narrow escape. Not content with dabbing on a bit of antiseptic, he had a hot bath and lathered himself with Carbolic soap.

Despite Japanese biological warfare, Clarence had escaped serious illness during his first year in China, but poor nutrition and hard work had taken its toll on him. When Clarence arrived from India in 1944, he was no longer a youth, not yet a man. His fair hair had glistened in the sunlight and he wore a tan—the colonial biscuit-coloured tan. Now his cracked mirror reflected a pale, pinched face above a bony frame—yellow from the mepacrine he took to protect himself from malaria.

In August 1944, at a meeting between Churchill and Roosevelt, the two leaders had agreed to concentrate all their resources to open up the Burma Road by constructing a highway from Ledo in India to Kunming, eleven thousand miles away.

On 28 January 1945, General Pick, the US general, cut the ceremonial tape separating the border from Burma into China. Firecrackers roared and popped from balconies, windows and streets when the general and his men arrived at the Western Gate of the city of Kunming.

Hostilities with Japan continued for another seven months after the American Mars Task Force and Stilwell's Chinese X force had linked the Ledo Road with the Burma Road. Clarence rejoiced. Now his task was over and he could return to his beloved family.

In mid-December, Doug wrote, informing Clarence that Eva's husband, Albert, was in Holland, and Roy was home on embarkation leave. His next letter took nearly three weeks to arrive, and contained news of a fourteen-pound goose for Christmas dinner at Anne and Stan's place. His letters now brought happy news.

By the end of May 1945, the war in Europe was over. Doug boasted he was to receive another couple of medals and would soon look like a bird of paradise with all his gongs.

'Our sergeant sent our water tanker driver to fill the tank with two hundred and fifty gallons of wine for the peace celebration,' he wrote.

By August, Doug was in transit to the UK on twenty-eight days' leave.

Delighted for his brother, who had fought so valiantly, Clarence longed to be home too. He yearned to see his family again.

Japan sued for peace on 14 August 1945. The next day, dozens of planes flew Kuomintang troops to the cities to take over from surrendering Japanese garrisons, and Chinese officials returned to their former capital, Nanking.

Clarence requested FAU headquarters for permission to leave his post at Kunming and fly to Shanghai. Now that the war was over, he hoped to get his discharge from the FAU and board a ship to England from there.

Within a fortnight after Japan's surrender, the US Fourth Squadron moved to Kunming, and by the middle of November, they departed for Shanghai. Clarence had made many friends among the airmen over a cup of tea or an iced coffee at the canteen, and, as he was on friendly terms with the crewmen, he asked them for a lift.

A pilot readily acceded to his wishes and flew him to Shanghai in one of the transport planes.

CHAPTER 22

SHANGHAI

China, 1945-1946

Clarence glanced down from the plane as it circled above Shanghai. The city stood at the mouth of the Yangtze with its famous landmark—the Bund, a kilometre-long walkway, running along the waterfront. The yellow waters of the river churned up with silt from up-country and spewed forth like treacle into the thirty-mile-wide jaws. A mass of sampans covered the sea.

The wheels hit the tarmac with a thud and the plane taxied to a stop. Clarence stepped out, put his fingers to his nose and blew hard. His eardrums cleared. He pushed his way through the hustle and bustle, clambered aboard the airport bus to the city centre and found a seat.

Trucks, trams, cars, rickshaws, jeeps, and pedi-cabs filled the air with a cacophony of sounds—blasting and beeping horns. Thousands dodged the traffic. Pedestrians, hawkers and beggars thronged the pavements. Big department stores offered exquisite silks and woollens in their shopfronts. Neon signs sparkled.

The bus dropped off all passengers at the terminus. Clarence collected his baggage and hailed a rickshaw. A coolie ran towards him, took his luggage and waited for Clarence to sit down and name his destination before he placed his hands on the two shafts. He set off at a run through the wide boulevards, the veins in his legs standing out like purple ropes entwining his muscles. He wove the rickshaw among other vehicles and kept up his pace until he stopped in front of the FAU office. Clarence handed him a coin, picked up his battered brown portmanteau and entered the building.

Staff were busy sorting out piles of correspondence and no one paid him the slightest attention until he cleared his throat. When one of the men looked up, he asked, 'Excuse me. Is there any mail for Clarence Dover?'

The man jerked his head in the direction of the receptionist, who sat tucked away in a corner. Clarence had not seen her at first because of the number of people crowding the cramped room. He walked over and repeated his question to her. She seized the mail, snatched an entry book out of a rack in front of her, flung it open and grabbed a pen. When he signed for the mail, she handed him two letters and an aerogramme from Doug.

Clarence thanked her and moved off to read his mail without intruding upon her time.

His brother had written the first letter on board a ship from war-torn Italy. He'd received twenty-eight days' leave before being sent off elsewhere. He was on his way home and expected to be there on September 20. Everyone was introspective, drawing closer to each other, talking of their hopes for the future.

The second letter was dated the twenty-first, saying that he'd arrived home from Italy. Their Dad, Eva, Stan and Ann had been there to greet him. Roy was home on leave. Nottingham looked much the same, he wrote. Most of the girls were still as innocent and sweet as ever, but some of them seemed to have lost all sense of decency. One of the neighbours had been running a house of ill repute and had a baby to prove it.

Clarence glanced at the doorway that had been left open. He put away the letters and once again, moved towards the receptionist. He had forgotten to ask whether she knew of someplace he could stay.

She shook her head. 'British and American servicemen have filled hotels to capacity so accommodation is difficult to find.'

As he continued to stand before her counter, she shrugged and rifled through a file. 'Here's one, if you don't mind sharing a flat with a family.'

She scribbled an address on a piece of paper and handed it to him.

He balked at the prospect of living with strangers, but he was desperate for a place and knew he couldn't afford a hotel.

Clarence hailed a rickshaw and read out the address of the flat. On his arrival, he discovered that a Japanese family rented the apartment. He recoiled at the thought of sharing an apartment with them, but they bowed in greeting. A few months ago, he'd have regarded them as the enemy, and even now, he found it difficult to control his anger, but he nodded and smiled. He flexed his fingers and a vein pulsed in his neck. He could not help wondering how many prisoners the man had subjected to torture. He checked himself. *Past injuries should be forgotten. He must forgive and forget.*

Clarence glanced out of the window. The sun shone brightly outside, so he didn't need his mackintosh. He left his things on his bed and headed for the Post Office, where he sent off a cable to Doug. Then he returned to his room and unpacked. The place was small, but under the circumstances, he was glad to have it.

After he had settled in, Clarence visited the prisoner of war camps around Shanghai, looking for anyone from Nottingham. His first visit was to Lunghua Camp where nearly two thousand Allied nationals had been imprisoned. The Red Cross still cared for the hundreds remaining there.

The surgeon, who had been an inmate under Japanese occupation, showed him around. Street signs hung askew, a rotting reminder of the past three years when British inmates had given them nostalgic names such as Piccadilly Circus and Lambert Lane.

Clarence's heartstrings tugged at him, filling him with an intense longing for home. Five years had passed since he had left Nottingham and, like a child seeking the warmth of his mother's arms, his thoughts turned to England. Someone had once commented that the Englishman thought he was only a little lower than the angels and a good deal more important, Clarence mused. This sense of pride had kept the internees alive during the war.

'Here's a list of names,' the surgeon said, startling him out of his thoughts.

Clarence scanned the pages, his heart beating fast in anticipation of seeing a familiar name, but none presented themselves. Relieved that no one he knew had been interned there, yet frustrated at being unable to help anyone, he handed back the list.

'I'll show you around.' The surgeon made a circuit of the camp and pointed to an open tract of ash and cinders. 'This is where we buried them. Without proper implements, we could only dig shallow graves in the hard ground.'

He paused and put a hand to his brow. 'Not all the dead have been accounted for. Many died on the death march or dropped off on the wayside.'

Clarence's shoulders sagged as he left with weary steps. Wrecks of Japanese aircraft lay strewn about, covered by dense vegetation. Nature had put in her claim, her tenacious claws clutching everything in her path. *How rapidly the jungle endeavoured to hide the ravages of war.*

He hailed a passing rickshaw back to the Bund where *HMS Belfast* lay at the docks, flying the White Ensign, waiting to ferry sick and dying British prisoners-of-war to hospitals in Hong Kong. Clarence showed his pass to the guard on duty. The officer-in-charge nodded, and allowed him to scan the list of survivors. He knew no one, but he walked among them, reading from his Bible to a dying man, and helping to write a letter for a soldier who'd lost his right hand.

In January 1946, the *HMS Belfast* sailed off, her mercy mission finally completed. Clarence hoped the old vessel might find peace during the aftermath of unrest that follows a war.

The day after his return from the camp, Clarence sat down to write home to Doug about the escalating prices of everything. He sealed and stamped his letter. Only when he had posted it, did he remember he'd forgotten to get in touch with his friend Parry before leaving Kunming. Perhaps he'd meet him here at Shanghai.

On the way back from the Post Office, he met Geoffrey McPherson, a Nottingham businessman. He'd been a pillar of strength to conscientious objectors during the war, organising regular meetings to help them with their problems.

'I'm making arrangements for exporting goods into China. What are your plans?' he asked Clarence.

'I'm still attached to the Friends, but I'm waiting to return home. As soon as I've seen as much as I can of China, I'll apply for a release and go back to Nottingham.'

Geoffrey smiled. 'What would you say to a job in my firm, based at Shanghai?'

'I'd be glad to earn some money again. The war has left me penniless. Of course, the FAU has always provided for me, but I need to put away a nest-egg for the future.'

'Houses are scarce at home,' Geoffrey said. 'Wouldn't hurt you to delay your return for a bit. See me at ten tomorrow and I'll fix something up for you.'

That night, Clarence wrote to Mary, asking her if she would wait for him if he took the job.

As soon as Mary saw the postmark on the letter, she raced to her room and sat breathless on her bed. She read it in an ecstasy of joy, and pressed it to her lips several times. After a few minutes, a composed and deliriously happy Mary penned a short note to Clarence. The letter stated that she'd wait as long as he wanted, although her heart ached for him. She ended by advising Clarence to act in the manner God inspired him. She understood him now, and knew he'd only be guided by the Lord.

Within a fortnight, Clarence received Mary's reply. He opened the letter in feverish haste, and read it through several times. He held the letter to his heart for a few seconds before putting it away in his wallet along with her photo. Then he applied for release from the FAU.

On 31 May 1945, Clarence received a memo releasing him from the obligation to undertake work for which he had registered. He had been a full-time voluntary member since October 1940.

The following day, a doctor checked his health. Clarence started to buckle his belt. He hesitated and with downcast eyes, said, 'There's something I'd like to ask you, Doc.'

The doctor laid his hand upon Clarence's shoulder. 'Fire away.'

'I've lived a puritanical life, and I'm engaged to be married, but am a bit worried.'

'No love pangs? Afraid you won't be up to it?'

Clarence flushed and compressed his lips.

'That's more common than you think. At stressful times and periods of enforced abstinence from sexual activity, this thought can enter one's mind. It's common among prisoners-of-war and during wartime. Don't fear. It's quite normal. You've nothing to worry about.'

Clarence sighed. 'Thanks, Doc.'

'Glad you mentioned it though. Just relax and you'll be all right.'

The doctor inoculated him against cholera, typhoid, typhus, plague and smallpox. They made Clarence ill for some days, so he took it easy. *Wouldn't do to be sick now, when there was so much to look forward to.*

Until late September 1944, FAU Headquarters remained at Kutsing, and Parry worked on the Kutsing-Luksien run. After the war, the town became isolated and the garage closed. He left for home in November 1945, but not before going to see Clarence in Shanghai.

Parry arrived like a tornado, talking non-stop of conditions in China. For a few minutes, it was impossible for Clarence to say anything.

'What do you intend to do?' he asked, when he was finally able to speak.

'Return via Calcutta and Bombay. Join Gray Peile and others from the FAU, then travel together.'

'Times are tough back home,' Clarence said. 'I'll be staying here for a while longer. I've got a job and am engaged to be married, you know.'

'You're a sly one, Dover. No wonder you've kept away from the native girls. Congratulations. Wish you all the best.'

'Do keep in touch.'

'I'll write from Bombay. Perhaps return with a bride.' Parry paused for a few seconds. 'Heard that a number of Free French who had remained in hiding began to suspect Pierre of spying and passed on the information to Allied Headquarters in Kunming.'

'I believe the Allies had dealt him summary justice,' Clarence said.

'Serves him right. He caused so many unnecessary deaths.'

A twinge of guilt shot through Clarence for not realising sooner that he'd befriended a spy. He blushed and averted his gaze from Parry.

After two or three months, Clarence received a letter from Parry complaining about the high prices of meals, the beat-up beds at a bed-and-breakfast, and the lack of toilets in Bombay. In a lighter strain, he mentioned going to *Hamlet*, starring John Gielgud in the title role.

His letter ended saying he'd met Barbara Hamilton from the Red Cross. She took him out for dinner several times before heading off to Denver.

Parry sailed back to the UK and arrived at Southampton in November 1945 after a ten-day trip from Bombay.

Clarence spent a busy year at Shanghai, working in Geoffrey's import-export business. At times, his job took him to the Jewish sector of Shanghai. The community had its own synagogues, schools, theatres, hospitals, clubs, cemeteries and publishing houses. Residents had come from Baghdad, Spain, Portugal and India since 1844, drawn there in search of business. Thousands of Jews had fled to Shanghai from Nazi persecution as it was the only place in the world where visas were not required.

One day as Clarence wound his way down the winding streets of the Hongkou District, he met Samuel, who gave him a brief run-down of their situation during the war. 'We've been more fortunate than most,' he said. As he spoke, his nostrils inflated, accentuating his pinched facial appearance. 'The Japs left us alone for a while, but as Hitler had put the pressure on their Allies in February 1943, the military closed our businesses and established an insulation section.'

'A concentration camp?'

Samuel shrugged. 'We had no barbed wire and were not heavily patrolled, but adults needed passes to go in and out.' He paused, biting his lip. 'We remained there for five hundred and sixty-one days until the Nazis surrendered in Europe. Out of thirty-one thousand of us, one thousand five hundred died from starvation and sickness.'

'Will you continue to live here?'

'I'll be moving to Israel before long,' Samuel replied.

Clarence smiled, glad to know that some Jews, like Samuel, managed to escape being interned in a concentration camp. He'd been unaware of all this, so he decided to find out a bit more at the Jewish quarter, but work kept him busy.

In winter, sleet and snow chilled him to the marrow, and fog often drifted in from the sea, causing traffic jams in the city. In summer, the heat was oppressive and humidity lay like a blanket, stifling his energy and enthusiasm. The air was still and sultry, but despite typhoon warnings, unable to confine himself indoors, Clarence went out for a stroll. Slowly, the sky darkened to dull, impenetrable lead. Black clouds gathered and a fork of blue flashed out, followed by the first crashing explosion.

Clarence hastened to the flat, tightened the hood of his mackintosh and fastened it securely. The wind tossed loose objects around and smashed down doors, forcing windows open. Trees bent sideways, scattering leaves and branches. Palms ducked their heads to invisible hands. Some sprang back in protest—others appeared like umbrellas blown inside-out. Lightning now played incessantly, the thunder echoing and re-echoing among the hidden peaks. Rain followed, first in large solitary drops, then in stinging darts. Finally, it poured down in sheets. Clarence had witnessed storms at sea on his trip out to India, but never one as angry as this. Clothes wringing wet, he staggered into the flat. The houseboy was busy sweeping a torrent of water that had flooded the hallway.

Clarence waded through the flood, which reached to the foot of the stairs. After a hot shower, he looked out from the solidly built windows, but sheets of rain obscured his view. He sat down and picked up the evening newspaper to catch up on the news.

The papers displayed photos of landslides, homes washed away and emergency personnel pulling out people trapped in wreckage. War again, but a battle of the elements.

Clarence offered up prayers for the victims and thanked God for keeping him safe and secure during the storm.

Mail from Doug kept coming in as soon as he returned to England on leave. The first letter informed Clarence that Stan and Ann were expecting a little Dover.

In October, Clarence wrote to Doug about his job at Shanghai. By then, Doug had been posted with the peace-keeping forces to Italy. He was stationed at Trieste, where the winds were so icy that if the truck was parked facing the wind, water froze despite the anti-freeze.

Doug replied straight away to his brother, saying that he didn't blame him for stopping at Shanghai instead of returning to Blighty and having to hang around before he could find a job. He also mentioned that Eva and Albert's baby was due in May.

In November, Doug went sightseeing in Venice. The city was alive with rats and bathing was forbidden as the canals were contaminated with plague and typhus germs. Venereal disease was prevalent in the city. It only cemented Doug's resolve not to date any of the local girls.

At Christmas, Doug had turkey, pork, pudding and mince pies, which were served in the traditional way by officers and senior non-commissioned officers. General Sir John Harding had come in to wish the men all the best.

Clarence cherished Doug's letters and replied as soon as time permitted.

China remained in the grip of a civil war between the Nationalists and Communists, with the Communists based at Yenan. In 1946, Geoffrey wrote to Clarence, ordering him to wind down the business as he intended to fly out and finalise things within the following month.

Knowing that his time in China was ending, Clarence took a trip up the Yangtze, Shanghai's main artery. The heat cast a haze over the land but when it lifted, he glimpsed the roofs of houses—some tiled, others covered with rush matting. All buildings ended in an upward curl like an oriental smile.

'Chinese believe evil spirits float around in the air and that the curled roof bounces them back into the atmosphere,' Bill had told him when he first arrived in China.

Passengers rigged up shelters to shade themselves as the heat increased. Mosquitoes savaged them, but fortunately, Clarence had taken his daily dose of mepacrine. His ears buzzed and he was sallow—almost like a native.

He travelled as far as the three gorges of the Yangtze, then took a boat back to Shanghai, knowing he'd never have the chance to visit China again. The river meandered along half the provinces of China, cut its way through mountains and flowed in a rich fertile plain before reaching the sea.

For two nights the wind had been cold, but now it turned hot again as they approached Shanghai. Clarence felt the pulse of humanity and stepped ashore, stretching his legs after the cramped conditions on board. A pagoda dominated the Bund, its roof shining under the morning dew. Then the smell of night soil and drains rose to greet him. The *Bouquet d'Orient*.

When his boss, Geoffrey McPherson, was due to arrive at Shanghai, Clarence met him at the airport. McPherson handed him a letter from Mary. 'I've a job for you based at Nottingham,' he said. 'I've made arrangements for you to return on a US freighter with port calls at Hong Kong, Kobe and the Philippines to San Francisco. You're to have a fortnight's rest there before returning to Nottingham. I'd like to put more meat on your bones before you return.'

Home. The word sounded so familiar and comforted Clarence in a way he hadn't felt in five years of absence. How fortunate he'd been to meet Geoffrey who had not only found him a job in Nottingham when he returned home, but was also giving him a month of rest and recuperation before his return. Until now, he hadn't considered that his appearance might worry Mary and his family.

He'd done his job and aided the war effort without killing a single person. He puffed his bony chest out in pride.

Recalling his desire to find out more of the Shanghai Jews, Clarence visited the Ohel Moshe Synagogue and asked to interview one of the rabbis who'd been in the Jewish ghetto during the time of Japanese occupation.

The rabbi looked pleased to grant him his request. A pair of large ears protruded from his face. He rubbed his left ear. 'Shanghai is known as the modern day "Noah's Ark". Most of us have left, so I'm unable to find a former resident for you to interview, but I'll fill you in as much as possible. Wealthy Jews from Baghdad have been living in Shanghai since the nineteenth century. Russian Jews came here after World War One to escape anti-Semitism and the Soviets. Those with money lived in the international quarters and created a settlement like a little Vienna with cafes, bakeries and Jewish schools. The next lot of refugees came from Germany and Austria in the 1930s, fleeing from Hitler and his Nazis.

'The wealthy Baghdadi Jews, the Kadoorie, Hardoons and Sassoon families, the Russian Jewish community and American Jewish charities helped provide shelter and food to those who lived in the ghetto. This source dried up, however, after the bombing of Pearl Harbour.

'The last batch here came from Poland and Lithuania in mid-1941. It's a pity you can't meet Nina Wertans. She was six when Germany invaded Poland. The family first fled to Vilnius, but the Soviets entered the country soon after. Hearing that the Japanese consul, Chiune Sugihara, was issuing transit visas for Jews via Japan, they applied for one. The family was only one of the three thousand Jews saved by him,' he said.

'Perhaps he realised what their fate would have been if they didn't escape,' Clarence said.

The rabbi nodded. 'They took a train to Moscow, then boarded the Trans-Siberian Railway to Vladivostok—a ten-day journey. Once there, they drove to Kobe in Japan, and went by boat to the French concession in Shanghai. It was the only place that would receive them.'

'How exhausting for them!' Clarence exclaimed.

'At least they managed to escape the death camps in Poland.'

Clarence remained silent, waiting for the rabbi to continue, but as he, too, stood in silence, Clarence asked, 'What was life like in the ghetto?'

'The family lived in comparative comfort until late 1943, but the Germans demanded that all stateless Jews be moved to a designated area. They then had to move to the Jewish quarter. Nina, being a child, was free to leave the area and play with her Chinese and Jewish friends. She attended a Jewish school with the best teachers and her father, who was an engineer, taught her geography, history, mathematics and literature. At the end of the war, at the age of fourteen, she left for California with her family. In fact, you've missed them by only a few months.'

'Fortunate girl,' Clarence muttered, thinking of the thousands of Jews who had died in the Holocaust.

'As more Jews arrived in Shanghai,' the rabbi continued, 'they were housed in large rooms with as many as a hundred beds. There were no walls, running water or toilets that flushed. It was different from the life they were used to, but they survived. But, some Chinese families were so poor that they often abandoned their babies on the streets. They were worse off than Jewish families.

'At the time, Japanese troops housed their soldiers in Hongkou, and one frequently saw a Japanese soldier killing the Chinese. They treated us a lot better than the Chinese as they probably thought we were a powerful group, and would help them in negotiating with the US after the war.'

Clarence thanked the rabbi heartily for giving him an interview, and left with a leaden heart.

The day finally arrived for Clarence's departure from China. On 5 July

1946, he climbed up the gangway of *SS General McMeigs*. He sensed a shiver of fear as he looked back, and a wave of pity swept over him as he glanced at the teeming mass of Chinese. He was returning to peace at home, but civil war still festered within China like a cancer about to break out again once the Allies departed.

He foresaw more trouble in store when Communists imposed their godless ways upon the people, and tried to undermine work done by Christian missionaries. Most of them had left—some bitter and others grieving.

Loneliness in this vast city took hold of him. He leaned on the ship's rail and watched the harbour lights slip by. Each mile brought him nearer too home.

CHAPTER 23

HOME SWEET HOME

Nottingham, September 1946

Clarence looked around his fellow passengers on the *SS General McMeigs*, but recognising no one, he strode to his cabin, aware of the crinkle of paper in his pocket. He always carried Doug's latest letter with him.

SS General McMeigs had served as a troopship during the war, and was now used as a repatriation ship. It had just transported over a thousand Japanese Canadians from a POW camp in Canada to the Japanese port of Uraga, south of Yokohama. Apart from the crew and the marines on board, the troopship carried thirty travellers of various nationalities—mostly English and French, with a couple of Poles, Germans and Chinese.

The voyage to San Francisco lasted a fortnight. When the ship touched in at the port, on 18 July 1946, friends from the FAU took Clarence on a tour of the city. From the Golden Gate Bridge, he contemplated the world-famous Alcatraz Island basking in the sunshine. Hours later, he stood at the bottom of Lombard Street, the most crooked road in the world, and gazed at it zigzagging between borders of flowers.

The following day at Fisherman's Wharf, he passed restaurants cooking deep sea crabs and other shellfish in cauldrons. The saline smell teased his nose.

Someone suggested he order half a crab. He did so, and waited to be served, wondering whether the dish would only suffice as an entrée. When dinner arrived, he marvelled at its size and knew it was sufficient to satisfy his voracious appetite.

Next day at Muir Woods, redwood trees cast a constant shadow on the forest floor. He barely caught a glimpse of the topmost foliage, and realised his American friends were not exaggerating when they had regaled him with stories of their hometowns.

Clarence spent the rest of his time visiting Alcatraz, riding a trolley and taking a drive down the coast. He pandered to his taste and sampled American food like hot dogs, corn muffins and casserole dishes with golden cheesy crusts. Later on, he haunted ice cream and chocolate shops, indulging himself. He'd swirl it around in his mouth, savouring the rich, creamy taste.

On his last day, Clarence said goodbye to all things Chinese at San Francisco's Chinatown. China had broadened his outlook but not his essential nature. He was twenty-seven now and more tolerant of other classes, races and religions. The rigid class system did not matter so much to him any longer. He recalled the time when an Indian soldier attempted to get into their crowded carriage and Angus had placed his booted foot against the doorway to prevent him from entering. He had felt pity for the Indian, but kept silent. Now, he would not hesitate to let the man in, regardless of class differences. After all, the poor chap was fighting on their side.

Sir Frederic Eggleston, Australia's envoy to China, had said, 'Amazing how the English were capable of living in a country and not altering one jot in their method of life.'

Clarence pondered over his words and agreed that although his attitude to others had changed, his own lifestyle hadn't.

Refreshed after his time in San Francisco, Clarence continued the rest of his six-thousand-mile voyage to New York via the Panama Canal. The banks swarmed with mosquitoes. The insects were enormous. Larger than any he'd ever seen. He recalled his bout of malaria and resolved to continue his daily dose of mepacrine while travelling. When he reboarded his ship, he shivered involuntarily, mistaking the hum of the motors for the humming of myriads of mosquitoes.

The 50.7-mile journey through the narrow isthmus from the Pacific to the Atlantic took over ten hours. As the ship went through the locks, Clarence gazed at the dense jungle that grew on both sides of the canal. Fort Clayton, built on fill from the excavation, arose before him. From there, the 33rd Infantry had ambushed Nazi U-boats and ensured the safe passage of bauxite ore, so vital to the aircraft industry. Even here, it was impossible to escape from memories of the violence.

He tried to shrug off all thoughts of war.

At New York, the sea reflected the grey sky. Waves rocked the ship and within minutes, Clarence received a drenching. He retreated to the safety of his cabin, removed his wet clothes and changed into warmer gear.

When the storm cleared, he returned to the upper deck. His heart lurched as the Statue of Liberty came into view. This is what he had longed for—the freedom to follow his conscience and to obey God's commandments without any compromise.

Customs and Immigration officials cleared him without much delay. He espied two members from the FAU holding a placard aloft and, lugging his much-travelled suitcase, he headed towards them. They shook hands and waited until all names had been ticked off. One of the men issued railway passes for Montreal and hustled them into waiting trucks. From there they were to board the *RMS Mauretania* for the final lap of their journey home.

At Montreal station, a Canadian member of the team met them and distributed boarding tickets stamped First Class. 'You'll be travelling in cabins with four bunks and you can dream of the thousands of Canadian war brides who have just vacated them.'

Clarence thanked him, glad they still looked after his welfare. Many other passengers travelled down in the hold.

The ship docked at Liverpool on 1 March 1946. He'd enjoyed the company and the food on board. Spring was in the air, and no amount of soot or smoke could blot out its welcomed freshness.

Clarence gulped down his first breath of England since leaving Liverpool like a long cool drink.

Then he leaned over the rails and studied the water. Peaceful. Only then, did he dare raise his eyes to gaze at the town that lay before him.

Fog came creeping up the Mersey from the Irish Sea, and tug boats plied the grey waters.

The sight of so many bombed and burned buildings smothered the joy of being in British waters once more. Blackened ruins remained where incendiaries had gutted them. Painful memories returned as he gazed at the destruction.

Through the mist, the Liver Buildings towered in majesty like a cathedral. He stared at the clock towers. *Legend says if the Liver birds fly away or die, the city will cease to exist.*

A cry of delight escaped him when his eyes alighted on the statue of the Liver birds on the tall structure.

Friends from the FAU home office shook hands heartily and gave him a railway pass to Nottingham. The station was crowded with women greeting others who also had been working overseas and were just returning to England, but Clarence had yet to meet his folk.

He took a train home, his heart hammering like a sledge-hammer. The minutes seemed to pass in fragmented pieces. People spoke to him. He answered mechanically; his thoughts were on Mary. *What would she look like?* He stared out of the window. *When would the train get into Nottingham?*

When the locomotive eventually steamed into the station he thrust his head forward, eager to meet his family after so long. His eyes widened, and his legs couldn't carry him fast enough to the bus stop. He could find his way blindfolded around the familiar streets. His forefathers had lived in the same street and suburb for generations.

Clarence boarded the bus. It had been raining and the big bluff of the Castle Rock was streaked with rain as it reared above the town. The River

Trent swept past under the bridge, and the grey sky glistened with silver here and there.

His lip trembled and he broke out in a cold sweat, thinking of his mother who always was the first to meet him whenever he returned from anywhere. The thought extinguished his joy of returning home. His shoulders hunched.

He alighted at the stop closest to his home. The streets were lit, and houses were speckled and spangled with lights.

When he finally arrived at his house, all the family was present. Mary was there too. Clarence folded her in his arms and breathed in her sweet fragrance. Joy swept across him like a surge of electricity. Every movement she made sent a hot wave through him.

It was some minutes before they withdrew.

Stan had remained at home in a reserved occupation, earning one pound per day plus overtime, unlike the poorly paid service men and unpaid members of the FAU. He welcomed Clarence as a hero.

Everyone laughed, revelling in sheer relief to be together again, even though the cloud of their dear mother's absence loomed in the background. Watson wiped his eyes while Eva poured tea from a set of Royal Albert of Country Rose design.

Where did his sister get them from? Clarence remembered his mother having to improvise by using jam jars when their cups broke and couldn't be replaced.

He brushed away all sad thoughts and smiled to himself, thinking of the first evening Eva's admirer, Albert Barker, had called in to take her to the cinema. She had used gravy browning on her legs and drawn a line up the back of her calves with her eyebrow pencil to make it resemble a stocking seam. That night, Eva had been in trouble for using the precious item to appease her vanity.

Mary stole away from the room, probably to let the family discuss family matters. Stan and Watson mulled over the local action and their losses.

More than five hundred high explosive bombs had fallen in Nottingham in May 1941 alone. Over two hundred people died, but most residents had sought shelter in the network of hand-carved sandstone caves during the raids.

Doug, Albert, Clarence and Roy swapped stories of life in uniform. Then, the talk turned to their war wounds. Eva's husband, Albert, had received a wound when a gun misfired. It had thrown him unconscious to the ground and killed the sergeant who was standing beside him. After a few stitches and some time in hospital, Albert had returned to fight the enemy. Now he flicked back a lock of his hair to reveal a neatly-healed scar on his forehead.

'Where did you get that?' Doug teased, 'Civvy Street?' Lifting up his trouser leg, he exposed his scars. 'Shrapnel,' he announced, beaming. 'Tore away the flesh.'

Although Clarence returned physically unscathed, he too had experienced the traumas of war. He lifted his shirt and pointed to his chest. 'A month ago you could see my ribs—left over from the malaria I got while trying to find a French spy's lair.' He looked up and blushed.

Mary had re-entered the room and was staring at his bare chest!

A few days later, Clarence boarded a bus, which took him past a cross-section of the city centre, as he wanted to see the changes in his home town. Furniture shops still lined Derby Road, and the red brick tenements that led to Market Square were the same. Angel Row on one side and the Town Hall on the other flanked the open square, where a transient population of pigeons still hovered among workers with their lunchtime sandwiches.

Clarence paused before Robin Hood's statue in the Nottingham Castle grounds and let his thoughts drift from their famous hero to more recent local ones. Admiral Sherbrooke, Captain of *HMS Onslow*, commander of an escort force to North Russia, stood foremost among Nottingham's heroes. He had lost an eye and was severely wounded during hostilities. Sherbrooke received the VC for gallantry in defending the convoy against odds at the Battle of the Barents Sea.

Major General Sir Robert 'Lucky' Laycock, another war hero, was chief of combined operations under Mountbatten. He achieved fame as a commando brigade officer in Libya when he shot his way into Rommel's desert headquarters.

Lieutenant Colonel Sam Derry was awarded a DSO for organising the Rome Escape Line for more than three thousand Allied servicemen.

Lieutenant Colonel Basil Ringrose, of the Sherwood Rangers Yeomanry, had commanded an army of twenty thousand Ethiopians and harried the southern flank of the Italian armies in the western desert. He too received a DSO.

Thousands of brave men from Nottinghamshire had fought for their country and many had left their bones in foreign lands. Conscientious objectors, too, had given their lives tending the wounded on battlefields.

Countless recollections thronged through Clarence's mind. He recalled his words to the tribunal that autumn day in 1940. *I've been brought up to believe that everything I do should be done as Christ would have done*, he had said. *He'd never kill a man. I cannot imagine Him holding a smoking rifle, or wiping a blood-stained bayonet.*

The war had tested Clarence in the crucible of tribulation. Now he could hold up his head as proudly as the rest and say, 'To save lives, I risked my own.'

EPILOGUE

Dear readers, since my story is based upon true stories of real people, I thought you might like to know what happened to some of your favourite characters. Clarence and Mary married in September 1948, and had two children, Mary and Paul. Clarence devoted his life to serving God and became a church minister.

His sister Eva and her husband, Albert Barker, moved to Portland, Australia soon after the war. They had two children—Colin and Sharon. Colin married Hazel, the author of this book.

A few years later, Doug married Barbara, and he and his wife joined Albert and Eva in Australia. Doug fathered three boys.

Clarence's friends, Angus and Albert, both resigned from the FAU. They married and settled down in their home towns.

Clarence never met Parry again. Parry remained with the FAU and worked in Bombay, India until 1947, when he left the Unit to study in the US. He visited Barbara Hamilton in Denver, settled down in the US, married and had three children.

Like so many others, Clarence could never forget the war years and kept in touch with his old friends by correspondence and through reunions.

www.ingramcontent.com/pod-product-compliance
Lightning Source LLC
LaVergne TN
LVHW041615070426
835507LV00008B/246